VEGAN FOR FUN

MODERN VEGETARIAN CUISINE
BY ATTILA HILDMANN

FOOD PHOTOS Simon Vollmeyer · **FOOD STYLING** Johannes Schalk · **PHOTOS** Sandra Czerny · **LAYOUT** Justyna Krzyzanowska

VEGAN

FOR FUN

"Every vegan meal helps both individuals and all of us. I simply want to get as many people as possible excited about vegan food."

ATTILA HILDMANN

INTRO
Not an I say so

When this book is finished, I'll have a long journey behind me. It all started when I was studying physics at university. My passion for cooking vegan food slowly turned into a profession. A few years later, I published my first cookbook myself. For this, I spent many nights on the internet researching how to photograph food; used some of my savings to buy a reflex camera, flashes, and a professional light table; and started to look into print design. The success of Vol. 1 was as overwhelming as it was unexpected. Vol.2 followed, and in 2010, I finished the trilogy with Vol. 3, which was awarded best cookbook of the year by the German Vegetarian Society.

When *Vegan for Fun* is completed and I'm holding a copy in my hands, it'll be one of the milestones in my life that really means something to me. After all, this is my first book that was produced professionally with every imaginable type of support that an author and cook could wish for. This is the final product that I stand for, the quintessence of my work: easy vegan recipes, short ingredient lists, and pure enjoyment—modern vegan cuisine without pointing a moral finger.

Veganism has long since lost its image of being a niche movement for weird people and is definitely on the rise, especially in health-conscious America. Many famous people are committed vegans and promote the vegan lifestyle: Oscar winner Natalie Portman, Bill Clinton, Mike Tyson, and Pamela Anderson, just to name a few. Veganism has developed from being a diet preferred by a minority into a movement that includes Hollywood stars, politicians, and athletes, and we will certainly see the same thing happen in other countries around the world. And science is on our side. A number of recent studies have shown that there's a strong connection between animal fat intake and lifestyle diseases and that our meat consumption is also partially responsible for the destruction of the rainforest, climate change, and the unchecked growth of livestock farming.

At the beginning of the 21st century, humanity is facing many challenges: the population is exploding and resources are becoming scarce. The planet's green spaces are continuing to shrink—as are the polar ice caps and the cage sizes for animals in factory farms. Many of us are not activists, and although I also don't count myself to be an activist, I do hope that with my recipes I can contribute to making a better world to leave behind for our children and grandchildren.

There are lots of things that speak in favor of a vegan diet, but healthy enjoyment is the most attractive thing for me: the taste and smell! It's easier than you think to be a successful vegan cook, and most importantly, it's a lot of fun! It's fun to be doing something good for yourself, and at the same time, to be helping to make a better world. And it's not about all or nothing. Every step in the right direction counts: one vegan meal per day or week—multiplied over a million people—would change more than you can imagine. I am convinced that this book can inspire many people and bring about a lot of change. It's always a question of what you know and what's available. If people see that it's possible to follow a delicious and cholesterol-free diet, then more and more people will do so. This book that you are holding in your hands contains more than ten years of experience and know-how in everything related to a vegan diet and cooking. Enjoy!

TABLE OF
CONTENTS

VEGAN FOR FUN: ENJOYMENT WITHOUT DOGMA

MY VEGAN LIFE

RECIPES

TIPS

Many good REASONS

Eating vegan foods has many substantial advantages—for all of us. It not only prevents lifestyle diseases, but beyond that it helps us to save our resources and to stop factory farming, the destruction of rainforests, and climate change, which are all things directly connected to our eating habits.

It's hard for us to imagine, but climate change and the melting polar caps are largely caused by livestock farming. The United Nations reports that livestock farming is responsible for 18 percent of the overall carbon dioxide concentration; the Worldwatch Institute believes it's more than 51 percent. Even if we assume that the figure is 18 percent, that's still more than the amount of carbon dioxide emissions produced by road, sea, and air transport together. This is because cows emit carbon dioxide (CO_2) and methane (CH_4)—both of which are gases that are very harmful to the environment. We could stop using all of our cars, planes, and ships tomorrow, and livestock farming would still be the worst climate killer. If polar bears were able to, they would surely take to the streets to protest against livestock farming. And the rainforests, our planet's green spaces, are also suffering massively from our high level of meat consumption. Huge areas of the rainforest are being cleared for cattle ranching and soy plantations. If you buy soy products instead of meat in the U.S., then you can be pretty certain that you're not supporting the destruction of the rainforests as all of the soybeans sold in the U.S. are grown there. In Europe, it's important to buy organic soy products as these are grown primarily in European countries, whereas their conventional counterparts are often grown on soy plantations where the rainforest was cleared. Vegan foods are also less of a burden on our resources: it takes about 6,500 gallons (25,000 liters) of water to produce 2 pounds (1 kilogram) of beef. Getting the nutrition we need by eating animals costs a lot of money, water, time, and resources. And let's be honest. None of us believe that factory farming is worth supporting, no matter whether that includes conditions such as abusive breeding practices, tiny cages, animal transports, or epidemics. When you eat vegan foods, you're taking a stand—and even with just one vegan day per week, you'll be looking beyond the edge of your plate—in the truest sense of the word!

A VEGAN
diet is cholesterol free

We live in a country, in which millions of dollars are invested in the treatment of cardiovascular diseases since many of us suffer from the long-term effects of having cholesterol levels that are too high. It's tragic just how many people have to suffer from these types of illnesses, and I don't mean just the patients, but also their friends and family. One reason, if not the main reason for this, is the excessive consumption of animal products that are high in cholesterol, which over a long period of time results in clogged arteries. Heart attacks then occur. The death of my father was one of the main reasons why I began to eat a vegan diet. I watched him die on what was supposed to be the first day of our skiing trip in Switzerland, and it was the darkest day of my life. My father always said that he wanted to enjoy life and good food. At the time, I wasn't yet a vegetarian or vegan and I was somehow helpless. The desperate attempts I made to forbid my father to eat his boiled egg on Sunday morning unfortunately didn't have any lasting success.

Likewise, my cholesterol levels were already too high when I was quite young. Even when I was eating a vegetarian diet, but not yet vegan, my cholesterol remained very high. The reason for this was that I topped every dish off with tons of cheese—parmesan on my pasta, French goat cheese on tomato salads, Gruyere melted on top of my Tomato Herb Baguettes. In the Asterix cartoons, you read that Obélix has superhuman strength because he had fallen into a pot containing a magic potion when he was a child. I must have fallen into a pot with cheese fondue; I don't have any other explanation for why I love good cheese so much. It was only when I cut out cheese and other dairy products—which is the most difficult part of becoming vegan—and began to live a vegan lifestyle that my cholesterol levels came down to a safe level and stayed there.

Cholesterol is important for our health, but our body produces enough cholesterol by itself. And those of us who consume too many foods high in cholesterol immediately increase our risk of getting the typical lifestyle diseases. Foods that contain a lot of cholesterol include crab, red and white meat, sausage, cream, cheese, and giblets. In contrast, the vegan foods that I eat are completely cholesterol free. Today, I know that it's too late for my father, but it's not too late for the millions or even billions of people in the world who are at risk for heart attacks or have even already had an operation and now have to take medicines such as beta blockers. There is a way out— and it will save us money and sadness, and it tastes amazing: vegan cuisine!

EASY
to supplement

A balanced vegan diet that only includes a little white sugar, but is rich in fresh salads, vegetables, and fruits and nuts—by the way, I'm a nut butter junkie—covers almost all of your body's nutritional requirements. It's important for vegans to get enough Vitamin B12, which is produced by microorganisms and doesn't occur naturally in plants. It's also important to get enough Vitamin D, especially in the winter months, as the body can only produce this vitamin with exposure to UV light. Your iron intake can also be too low. When I started eating a vegan diet, I was a "pudding vegan" and was subsisting on things like pasta made from white flour, cola, and soy ice cream. As a result, my hair started to get thinner. Since being bald by the time I was 25 didn't really seem so great, I began to search for a solution.

The solution was quite simple: I increased my iron intake because it's a key mineral for strong hair. Lentils, sesame seeds, nuts, and parsley contain a lot of iron, and when combined with Vitamin C, iron is more readily absorbed by the body. So, my simple pasta became lentil Bolognese pasta topped with parsley pesto and together with a glass of orange juice, this makes for a meal with a great amount of iron.

If you are planning on following a vegan diet, you do need to make sure that you are getting enough of a few specific nutritional components. Of course, this is also true for people who eat meat, but don't follow a healthy and balanced diet.

With products like enriched cornflakes and soy milk or nutritional supplements, it's easy to add some of these components to your diet. Of course, it isn't natural to take supplements, but it's something most people do frequently, without even realizing it, for example, by using iodized salt. But what is really natural today? We live in a highly industrialized world with many challenges: emissions, particulate matter, higher levels of UV radiation due to the vanishing ozone layer, and convenience food that is low in vitamins and minerals.

We even give our house plants a "multi-vitamin" occasionally when we fertilize them. I know that I should do the same thing for myself every now and then, especially in today's busy world. I believe that it's much better to be vegan and take a vitamin now and then than to take medication later for the treatment of a stroke or heart attack caused by the typical lifestyle diseases that are directly related to the intake of animal fats.

In addition, a vegan diet can significantly help lower the risk of cancer. Many fruits and vegetables have been scientifically proven to help lower this risk, for example, vegetables from the cabbage family, tomatoes, green tea, soy products, turmeric, and berries. All of these are now part of my weekly diet.

I spend a lot of time reading scientific literature on the topic of nutrition, and so often I read the same thing: eat less meat and animal fats and instead eat more fruits and vegetables because they are rich in antioxidants and polyphenols. It doesn't matter if you are doing it for anti-aging purposes, cancer prevention, or for strengthening your immune and cardiovascular system. Even though the latest insights regarding nutrition are sometimes contradictory, I don't think my doctor will ever tell me, "Attila, the latest scientific studies suggest that people need to eat more meat and animal fats. I'm going to give you a prescription for one hot dog per day so that you can quickly get healthy."

START
vegan

I've never thought that I was better than other people simply because I have different eating habits. In fact, it's much easier to start the project of eating vegan and healthier without thinking about any world-improving ideologies or goals.

In the beginning, the desire to live with awareness should be central. I now really enjoy being a conscious shopper and admit that I've almost turned into a shopaholic. But not for clothes. I love shopping in and browsing through organic grocery stores and farmer's markets. It's great because I always discover new things, for example, new tofu or nut butter varieties or fruits and vegetables that make my menu more interesting.

Make time for yourself for one whole day, let's say a Saturday that is really laid back—and eat only vegan foods on this day. This will mean trying out new things and slowly getting more familiar with eating vegan. Maybe you'll start your day with muesli topped with fresh fruit and some soy milk in your coffee. A fresh roll with jam or vegan hazelnut spread also makes for a great breakfast. There are also lots of other hearty vegan spreads to choose from. The beginning of your adventure should be really laid back.

Then think about what you especially like to eat for dinner and whether or not there might not be a vegan alternative. Start by enjoying shopping and preparing your meals, and also enjoy the opportunity to have a really healthy day!

It's not about having to eat 100 percent vegan, but rather simply about getting started. You might think that you're not really accomplishing anything. But that's just not true. Even if you only eat a vegan diet one day a week, you'll still be doing a lot for your own health. You'll be decreasing your cholesterol intake by about 15 percent and your body will have less work breaking down animal products.

If everyone on earth decided to do this, it would go a long way to conserve our natural resources and be much more effective than all the dogged talk about improving the world. Fifteen percent is much more than a proverbial drop in the ocean. And it's no longer a hidden fact that it's the excessive global consumption of meat and dairy products that has led to the constant expansion of arable land for the purpose of growing food for livestock. This has consequences for the environment that are constantly becoming more serious as a result of deforestation, over-fertilization, and methane emissions from cattle.

And maybe you won't stop at one day a week. Maybe you'll make it two regular days a week or—you might even not like to think about it— maybe three, four, or at some point even seven.

MY VEGAN LIFE

How everything STARTED

Every success story begins with one small step. I never would have thought that I would become well known as a vegan chef. I grew up in a family that placed a lot of value on good food. My mother was an au pair in France and raised my brother and me with good French cooking. My father was an engineer and avoided the kitchen like the plague. Surprisingly, he was the one who wanted me to become a cook when I was young. At the time, I didn't take the idea at all seriously; I was more interested in dreams of becoming an astronaut or a pilot.

Ideas about eating vegetarian or even vegan didn't play a role in the first 19 years of my life. I knew that there were vegetarians, but I hadn't met very many, and definitely wasn't interested in the topic. And why would I have been—meat tasted good and anyway, the cows in the commercials for milk looked to be doing quite well.

One day, when I was about 19, I ran into an old friend. We made plans to go see a movie together. And after about five minutes, he handed me a booklet on vegetarianism and began to tell me how a vegan diet made him feel good and that it was good for the planet and the animals, too. I was surprised to see how he had changed. It was really interesting; he explained everything without pointing any fingers and made me want to find out more about a vegetarian diet. Sometimes, life is like that: it's the chance encounters and short conversations that steer our lives in directions we had never imagined. We parked near the zoo in Berlin to go to the Zoo Palast movie theater, and as we got out of the car, I said, "Hey, Ahmed, I'm hungry. Let's go get a döner (see p. 40)! "Ouch! He looked at me and said, "Hey, Attila, I just told you about all of the problems that eating meat causes and now you want to go wolf down a döner?" We exchanged a meaningful look, and then I said, "OK, I'll do it. Starting today, I'm going to be a vegetarian!" On this first day, it meant that I wouldn't have a döner, but would instead go with a falafel—which is also tasty!

When I was still eating meat, I weighed 231 lbs (105 kg): I was overweight and lacked motivation.

Today—as a vegan—I weigh 154 lbs (70 kg): I'm in top physical shape and full of energy.

It wasn't until the next day that I realized what I had taken upon myself. No more döner, fried chicken, Big Macs, or steak—unimaginable! And no matter from which side I tried to embrace this idea, it seemed impossible.

The panic that I had began to fade when I went to an organic grocery store to stock up on sandwich spreads. It seemed like they had a wide variety of products. There's an organic grocery store not too far from where my family lives, where I'd been with my mother when I was a young kid. Back then, I got pretty excited about the free lotion samples, the smell of the whole grain rolls with raisins, and the friendly employees who often chatted with my mother for hours or for what seemed like hours. It was a different world.

After 19 years of French cuisine and totally unabashed enjoyment of junk food, I seemed to have found my way back to a healthy diet and the organic grocery store of my childhood. And a junk food diet was really an understatement: I loved the fast-food burger chains. No wonder then that my first attempts to cook on my own were limited to packaged soups and noodles with pasta sauce out of a jar.

In the beginning, my mother was worried about whether or not I would really stay healthy with my new vegan diet, and she thought about how I might improve and add to what I ate. She thought it was just a short phase that would soon pass. But I stuck with it and enjoyed it more each day. I could sense that I was suddenly lighter and full of energy—it felt really good!

A couple of months later, I knew a lot more about eating vegan. You just replace dairy products with plant-based alternatives such as soy, oat, or rice milk, soy yogurt, and Italian rice milk ice cream. At that time, the selection wasn't yet very large and soy milk wasn't available in the big supermarkets, but I was able to get everything I needed in organic grocery stores. Today it's easier than it's ever been.

At the beginning, protecting the animals was the most important reason for me. I found it unbearable that the chickens were kept in cages, and terrible that cows were impregnated so that they would produce milk and that their calves were seen as a surplus by-product.

Over the next few years, many more important aspects of a vegan diet became evident: health, the climate, the environment, poverty in developing countries, and my cholesterol level, which had consistently been too high because I ate too many dairy products and eggs.

After completing school, I went to university and as a way to balance the demanding mental strain, I found myself more and more often in the kitchen. It was fun. I always had something good to eat even though I had a small budget and earned less than most people. And actually, I still had enough money to bake vegan chocolate cakes for parties, where they got lots of "Oohs!" and "Aahs!"

At some point, I realized I wanted to share what I had learned. I wanted to help people realize that the ideas they have about vegetarians and vegans are just clichés. I myself had also harbored huge prejudices about a vegan diet that didn't disappear until I had my first successes cooking vegan. I published my very first recipes on a website, and seven years later, my cookbooks followed. And after they were released, I appeared on stage, and had sponsor contracts, interviews, and TV appearances. Now, my fourth cookbook *Vegan for Fun* is finished, and I have a good feeling that it has the ability to get a lot of things going—for the planet and for my career. I'm excited to see what will happen next!

Doctrines are OUT

I was a vegetarian for a long time. When I first started to research the topic of veganism, I usually ended up on scary vegan websites. Here, people who eat meat and also vegetarians were wildly accused of being "murderers", and much of their rhetoric smacked of militant aggression.

I suddenly really wanted to go to my favorite Italian restaurant and order a Canadian bacon pizza with extra cheese or tagliatelle with lots of cream sauce. If these food extremists didn't believe I was doing anything to improve the world as a vegetarian, then why should I hold back at all? That was the way I thought back then. But this didn't keep me from wanting to find out more about the topic. The arguments were all on the table: a vegan diet was good for the climate, the animals, and my health. My own veganism was, at first, focused solely on diet.

When I'm at a shoe store, I sometimes buy running shoes that are partially made of leather because the selection of vegan athletic shoes is still very limited. When I say something like this on the radio or on TV, many rather confrontational vegans are always outraged. A partial success seems to be more threatening to them than total failure. I don't believe you can reduce a person down to their leather shoes or the foods they eat, but many extreme vegans do think this way. I was never the type that felt convinced of anything when I saw animal-rights activists in the city center who were covered with fake blood and armed with megaphones. When I see adults wearing cow costumes and holding up signs that say "Meat is murder," I smirk inside and ask myself, what they are trying to accomplish. The few hate mails I've received have been from vegans. Up to now, not a single meat eater has complained that I'm trying to offer light and delicious cholesterol-free alternatives.

What makes me really sad is this "I'm a better vegan than you" phenomenon. Almost like in a cult, people aren't convinced that you are truly vegan until they examine everything: are there any nonvegan items in your household or do you still own any items like down comforters, wool sweaters, or leather shoes. Whoever has to admit to something here, is no longer worthy of being called a vegan.

That would be like demanding that anti-nuclear activists throw away all energy wasters including light bulbs, cars, and refrigerators.

Looking towards success, I believe that it works much better if you are relaxed about the whole thing and have fun with it. After all, every long journey begins with a small step. The goal that you are working towards and whether or not you want to take breaks on your journey should be up to you! It's up to me whether or not I'll ever eat meat or other animal products again—I don't know if I will and I want to leave it at that. I'm doing great cooking vegan and I feel totally healthy. And I'm doing it for me and for a better world and I'm not going to let people rope me into anything.

However, I do want to make it clear that in general, I feel a strong connection to vegans and vegetarians, and their lifestyle; they deserve a lot of respect for acting responsibly with regards to the environment and our resources.

My views on
FITNESS

I'm not a fan of synthetic protein shakes, thick necks, or gyms overrun by muscle heads. I believe that you should work out without overdoing it, eat fresh and colorful foods, and give your body enough time to recover. My workout plan serves primarily to increase my feeling of well-being. Nothing is better than taking a hot shower after my morning run through the forest, which included stops for situps and push-ups, and afterwards, starting my day with a delicious pancake breakfast.

When I spend time on fitness forums, I'm always astonished by the obsessive discussions about eating and training. I come across questions such as "How much meat do I have to eat in order to get my x grams of protein?" Apart from the fact that most of us in Western countries consume too much protein, which overworks our kidneys, I don't think much of the words "have to." I eat when I'm hungry, and sometimes when something looks really good.

These days, even children and teenagers are in front of the computer way too much, they are often overweight (I was also addicted to the internet and overweight when I was young), and many develop problems with their posture. Physical activity and exercise are crucial. You don't have to start by training for a marathon. It's best to just start slowly. At some point, you'll realize that you have fun increasing the difficulty and challenging yourself.

I find it important to do good endurance training: I go swimming, cycling, or running several times a week, and do weight training once or twice a week. Twelve to fifteen repetitions are enough, particularly for women who don't want to end up looking like Arnold Schwarzenegger. After my workout sessions, I give myself the time I need until my body feels ready to train again. This way, I'm able to constantly be improving my performance.

It's really important to start everything slowly and safely so that your body can get used to exercising. You'll get healthy by eating in moderation, enjoying your food, and working out!

VEGAN 2.0
Facebook & social networks

The internet is really a great thing when you know how to use it productively. There are a lot of helpful and informative websites, for example, for the vegetarian associations in your own country. There, you'll often find the most current and important information about new products and a vegan lifestyle, and you can take part in forum discussions. For instance, the German Vegetarian Society not only works to make vegetarian dishes more popular, but also does a lot to promote a vegan diet. Sebastian Zösch, the current manager, is a good friend of mine whom I've cooked together with on more than one occasion. He's also vegan to the core.

You can also find vegetarian associations on Facebook and actively take part there. And if that's not enough for you, you can start your own Facebook group or start a forum based on tolerance for vegans and those interested in veganism—unfortunately, there are very few of these out there today.

If you want to get your body in shape and exchange ideas with other athletes, have a look at www.veganbodybuilding.com. There, you'll come into contact with amateur and professional athletes who eat a vegan diet. These athletes aren't tired all the time and are the picture of health.

Or if you travel a lot and are often in different countries, then you can use www.happycow.net to find local vegan restaurants—so that you don't have to starve. Even in the most remote places in the world, it seems like there's often a vegan restaurant or café to be found.

Use the internet to show your friends and followers how tasty and delicious vegan food is, and try starting your own blog. This is how my success story started in 2003. And then a few years later, I started uploading my own cooking videos to YouTube. You can find my videos at www.youtube.com/TheFreshVegan, and if you do a little looking around on YouTube, you'll also find other interesting and inspiring vegan cooking channels. It has never been easier to network globally with other people who have similar views and interests. Use the internet for the vegan cause.

RECIPES

Kitchen
BACKSTAGE

When years ago, I decided to eat exclusively vegan, I was somewhat disappointed with the recipes I found on the internet and in some cookbooks. I hadn't even been very impressed by the vegetarian recipes I had tried out that at least had the bonus of having cheese, cream, or quark on top, which helps to make many dishes tastier.

Over the years, I developed my own recipes, which in many cases, took a lot of time. My Bolognese sauce is a good example. All of my friends like it, and it's become a true hit in the world of vegan cooking. When I look back, I see how the sauce transformed over the years from a wobbly tofu tomato soup into a really tasty Bolognese. That's just how it is: everything takes time!

I'm happy to share my tricks and experiences with you because then it will be easy for you to avoid many typical mistakes that people make at the beginning. Let's start with **TOFU,** which is really something you can't do without. If you want to use tofu as ground beef, then you can mash it with a fork, and you should fry it separately in an ample amount of olive oil—only by doing this, does the wobbly consistency disappear. If you want to use tofu to make chili or Bolognese, just put the tofu in a skillet and fry for 10 minutes. Then add the onions and other ingredients such as tomatoes, fresh herbs, and most importantly red wine, a lot of red wine! For years, I did it in the other order, but tofu is simply not like ground beef. The amazing thing about tofu is its ability to transform. Tofu is really versatile. Many people don't like the neutral taste, but that's exactly one of the advantages of this white miracle block, which, by the way, contains all eight essential amino acids! You can use tofu to make savory dishes as well as desserts, and it works well for Italian, Indian, American, or German style foods. After seasoning, you'll be rewarded with an amazing taste experience.

I also searched for many years for an alternative to dairy ice cream that would be equally delicious. It does work really well to use **SOY WHIPPING CREAM,** but the absolute best thing is my Cashew Vanilla Ice Cream, which is healthier and amazingly also soy free. But it still tastes incredibly creamy. And it only takes 2 minutes to make—I'm not kidding! It is however necessary to have a powerful blender with a tamper that makes it so nothing sticks to the sides of the blender. For years, I had used a really powerful blender without a tamper, and I always had the problem that the peanuts, pistachios, and other solid ingredients would stick to the sides. Each time, I would have to turn the blender off, scrape the sides, and then turn it back on. One time, I was scraping the sides with a spoon while mixing

(Do not try this!), and then I accidentally dropped the spoon. There's no need to worry since you can see that I still have both eyes, but the spoon burst through the glass and flew about 15 feet (5 meters) into the other corner of the kitchen. So, a blender with a tamper is definitely better. The Cashew Vanilla Ice Cream has a creamy consistency similar to that of vanilla ice cream made from cow milk, and you can fine tune it by adding chocolate pieces, candied walnuts, or—for those of you who are really brave—matcha green tea.

I admit that I love junk food. I'd do almost anything for French fries with ketchup and mayo or crispy tofu nuggets served with remoulade, which is similar to tartar sauce. I asked myself for some time how you could make a vegan **MAYONNAISE** or remoulade. At some point, though, the question became irrelevant because there are actually really good plant-based versions of mayonnaise available, for example, in organic grocery stores or in the organic section of many supermarkets. However, when I knew I would be cooking at university cafeterias for about 1000 students on multiple occasions as part of special vegetarian weeks, I had to figure out how to make mayonnaise in large quantities as cheaply as possible. The basic ingredients are plant-based milk, canola oil, mustard, sea salt, black pepper, and lemon juice. And the key ingredient is **GUAR GUM,** a vegetarian thickening agent, which can be found in many industrial food products, especially low-fat products. A small teaspoon is all you need to get about two cups of vegan mayo to thicken. I was able to use this recipe to make my beloved Big Mac sauce from my junk food days, and it works great.

In June 2010, I was on a television show, and as part of a test, I was supposed to make tofu burgers for a football team. Since the tofu was supposed to taste like meat and I didn't want the burgers to crumble on the grill, it took me a few weeks to get the recipe just right. I used a good barbecue seasoning, mustard, onions, and fresh herbs to get the tofu patties to taste meaty, and I used **LOCUST BEAN GUM** to get them to hold together on the grill. The football players didn't even realize that it was tofu and thought instead that they were eating conventional meat. And they thought that the true meat burgers that had been prepared at the same time were organic burgers. This was another indication that plant-based products are truly versatile. You just have to reach into your bag of tricks!

I often see panic in people's eyes when I tell them that I'm vegan. I have the feeling that many of them are expecting that I am going to zealously try to convert them and be accusatory. These stereotypes are unfortunately much too widespread. And I admit that I was exactly the same when I was still eating meat. At the time I had a girlfriend who was a vegetarian. When she was invited to come over to my family's house to cook and eat together, she prepared a carrot stew, while I made turkey drumsticks with dumplings and red cabbage for my family. During the meal, I looked at her plate and felt a bit sorry for her, and I was happy that I could sink my teeth into some juicy meat.

After seeing the sad-looking carrot slices in my girlfriend's stew, becoming a vegan was completely out of the question. What would I eat as a vegan? No meat, fish, eggs, or dairy products, and many vegans don't even eat honey.

What does that leave? You can't just go the whole day eating only fruits and vegetables. And you would definitely not feel full on that kind of diet! At least that's what I thought before I discovered my passion for vegan cooking. The following recipes are so delicious and nourishing that you won't miss anything. And no one needs to worry about having to eat bland carrot stews!

REALLY
satisfying

Attila's Spaghetti
WITH TOFU BOLOGNESE

INGREDIENTS for 2 servings

9 ounces tofu (250 g)

1 onion

2 garlic cloves

3½ tablespoons olive oil (50 mL)

4 tablespoons tomato paste

⅔ cup dry red wine (150 mL)

9 ounces durum spaghetti (250 g)

Sea salt

5.5 ounces tomato pureé (150 g)

1–2 teaspoons agave syrup (or raw cane sugar)

1 teaspoon dried oregano

Freshly ground black pepper

1 bunch basil

⅓ cup pine nuts (50 g)

¼ cup nutritional yeast flakes (50 g)

AH! "Rule number one for tofu: fry it well so that the wobbly consistency disappears. Be careful. For this recipe, it's essential that you do everything in the correct order. If you reverse the order and add the red wine to the tofu before adding the tomato paste, the sauce will turn violet instead of red."

PREPARATION TIME: 25 minutes

Mash the tofu with a fork. Peel and finely chop the onion and garlic cloves. Heat the olive oil in a saucepan and fry the tofu approx. 5 minutes, stirring often. Add the onions and sauté for 2 minutes. Then add the garlic and sauté for an additional 2 minutes. Add the tomato paste and cook for 2 minutes while stirring. Deglaze with red wine and cook for 4 minutes allowing the sauce to thicken. Cook the spaghetti according to the package instructions in an ample amount of well-salted water until the spaghetti is al dente. In the meantime, add the tomato pureé, agave syrup, and oregano to the spaghetti sauce. Allow to simmer for 3 minutes, and then season with salt and pepper. Wash the basil, spin dry, finely chop the leaves, and then fold into the sauce. Allow the spaghetti to drain in a sieve. Place on plates with the Bolognese. Toast the pine nuts for 3 minutes in a dry skillet and grind ⅔ of the pine nuts together with the nutritional yeast flakes and a little sea salt to a powder in a blender. Sprinkle over the pasta and garnish with the remaining pine nuts.

TEX-MEX BURGERS
with Guacamole and Salsa

INGREDIENTS for 2 servings

Tofu Burgers:

10.5 ounces tofu (300 g)

2 onions

½ bunch flat-leaf parsley

⅓ cup canned corn (50 g)

¾ cup canned kidney beans (50 g)

½ cup breadcrumbs (60 g)

2 level teaspoons sea salt

2 teaspoons paprika

2 teaspoons tomato paste

1 level teaspoon locust bean gum
(If not available, you can use guar gum.)

Freshly ground black pepper

¼ cup vegetable oil (70 mL)

Salsa:

2 tomatoes (approx. 250 g)

1¼ cups kidney beans (200 g) (can)

2 tablespoons chopped cilantro
leaves

2 tablespoons tomato paste

2 tablespoons olive oil

½ red chili pepper

1 tablespoon freshly squeezed
lemon juice

Sea salt

Freshly ground black pepper

Guacamole:

1 avocado

1 teaspoon freshly squeezed
lemon juice

Sea salt

Freshly ground black pepper

In addition:

Lettuce for the burgers

2 sesame buns

1 cup tortilla chips (30 g)

PREPARATION TIME: 60 minutes

For the burgers, mash the tofu with a fork. Peel the onions. Wash the parsley, shake dry, and purée together with the onions in a blender. Rinse off the corn and kidney beans and allow to drain. Combine all of the ingredients for the burgers, except for the vegetable oil, and knead well for 2 minutes. Then form 3 burgers from the mixture (the flatter they are, the more crispier they will turn out). Heat the oil in a skillet and fry the burgers for 2 minutes on each side over high heat. Reduce the heat to medium and fry the burgers an additional 4 minutes on each side until golden brown.

For the salsa, wash and dice the tomatoes. Mix together with the other ingredients for the salsa. For the guacamole, peel the avocado and remove the pit. Purée the pulp together with the lemon juice in a blender. Season with sea salt and pepper. Wash the lettuce and spin dry. Cut open the sesame buns and toast them for just a minute. Place the lettuce and the burgers on the bottom half of each bun, and then add the salsa, tortilla chips, and guacamole. Put the other half of the bun on top.

AH! "A TV show once gave me the task of making burgers for a football team so that they wouldn't notice that they were eating tofu instead of meat, and the whole thing was filmed live. Locust bean gum was the answer to my problem of how to give the burger mixture a texture similar to meat. The football players really thought that my tofu burgers were regular meat burgers. It's just a question of using the right seasoning and ingredients."

DÖNER

INGREDIENTS for 2 servings

Döner:

7 ounces seitan (200 g)

3½ tablespoons olive oil (50 mL)

2 teaspoons gyros seasoning

Sea salt

2 pieces flat bread (e.g., pita bread)

¼ head of green leaf lettuce
(lollo biondo, if it's available)

1 cup red cabbage (100 g)

1 onion

1 tomato

¼ cucumber

Sauce:

½ cup plain soy yogurt (100 g)

1 teaspoon curry powder

1 teaspoon ground paprika

2 teaspoons tomato paste

2 tablespoons vegan mayonnaise

1 tablespoon agave syrup

1 tablespoon freshly squeezed
lemon juice

Sea salt

AH! "Seitan has a nice texture
and is a favorite substitute for
meat. It's made from wheat
gluten and originated in Asia,
where it was developed by
vegetarian monks. Seitan is
perfect for this döner recipe!"

PREPARATION TIME: 15 minutes plus
10 minutes cooking time

Preheat oven to 400°F (200°C). Cut seitan
into paper-thin slices, approx. 1–1½ inches
(3 cm) long. Heat olive oil in a frying pan
and fry seitan for about 3 minutes on each
side. Don't fry it too long because seitan
gets chewy very quickly. Season with gyros
seasoning and sea salt. In a hot oven, heat
flat bread for 10 minutes until it is crispy.
In the meantime, wash the lettuce, spin it
dry, and tear into small pieces. Wash the red
cabbage and then cut into fine strips. Peel the
onion and cut it into paper-thin rings. Wash
the tomato, peel the cucumber, and cut both
into fine slices. Mix all the ingredients for the
sauce. Cut the flat bread in half and then slice
each half open. Spread some of the sauce on
the inside. Place a few lettuce leaves onto the
bottom half of the flat bread, and then add the
red cabbage, seitan, onion rings, and tomato
and cucumber slices. Pour the remaining sauce
on top of everything and cover with the top
half of the flat bread.

WILD GARLIC GNOCCHI
with Mushrooms in an Almond Cream Sauce

INGREDIENTS for 2 portions

1 medium-size potato (200 g)

Sea salt

⅓ cup first clear flour (40 g)
(If not available, you can use bread flour.)

1 rounded tablespoon corn starch

½ bunch wild garlic

1⅓ cups sugar snap peas (140 g)

2 tablespoons vegetable

margarine

2 sun-dried tomatoes without oil

1 red onion

8 ounces seasonal wild

mushrooms (230 g)
(e.g., white mushrooms, porcini, and chanterelles)

5 tablespoons white almond butter

Freshly ground black pepper

Oregano leaves

AH! "Sugar snap peas are delicately
sweet and tender and only need
to be blanched very briefly. But be
careful at the grocery store not to
get them mixed up with pea pods!"

PREPARATION TIME: 40 minutes

Peel the potatoes, cut into thin slices, and then cook
in well-salted boiling water approx. 10 minutes. Drain
the potatoes and either press through a potato ricer
or mash and knead until the mixture is smooth.
Fold in the flour and corn starch. The dough should
be fluffy, but shouldn't stick to your hands. Wash
and chop the wild garlic and knead into the potato
dough with ½ teaspoon of sea salt. Then let the
mixture sit approx. 5 minutes. Dust your work
surface with flour and roll out the mixture until it's
about ⅓ inch (1 cm) thick. Then cut into pieces about
⅓ inch (1 cm) thick and lightly press each piece with
a fork to get the classic gnocchi ridges. Allow the
gnocchi to cook in boiling salted water, until the
pieces float to the surface. In the meantime, cook the
sugar snap peas in salted water for 10 minutes. In
a skillet, sauté the sugar snap peas in 1 tablespoon
of margarine. Cut the sun-dried tomatoes into fine
strips. For the almond cream sauce, peel and finely
chop the onion. Wash and clean the mushrooms,
and then slice. Heat 1 tablespoon margarine in a
skillet and sauté the onions. Add the mushrooms
and sauté for approx. 5 minutes. Mix the almond
butter with ½ cup (120 mL) of cold water and add to
the mushrooms. Season with sea salt and pepper.
Arrange the gnocchi, sugar snap peas, mushrooms,
and sun-dried tomatoes on plates and garnish with
the oregano leaves.

BAKED POTATOES,
Tzatziki, and Green Beans with Thyme

INGREDIENTS for 2 servings

Tzatziki:

½ cucumber

3 garlic cloves

2¼ cups plain soy yogurt (500 g)

1 tablespoon olive oil

1 tablespoon white wine vinegar

Sea salt

Freshly ground black pepper

Tofu Bacon Cubes:

5.5 ounces smoked tofu (150 g)

1 tablespoon olive oil

Sea salt

Freshly ground black pepper

Baked Potatoes:

2 large potatoes

Green Beans with Thyme:

2⅓ cups fresh green beans (300 g)

Sea salt

½ bunch thyme

1 onion

2 tablespoons olive oil

Freshly ground black pepper

PREPARATION TIME: 45 minutes plus 60 minutes grill or bake time

For the tzatziki, peel the cucumber and use a slicer to cut into paper-thin slices. Peel the garlic and pass it through a garlic press. In a large bowl, whip the soy yogurt with a whisk until it is creamy. Fold in the olive oil and white wine vinegar. Stir in the garlic and cucumber slices. Salt and pepper. For the Tofu Bacon Cubes, cut the smoked tofu into small cubes. Heat the olive oil in a skillet and fry the smoked tofu for 3 minutes over high heat, stirring occasionally. Season with sea salt and pepper. For the baked potatoes, wash the potatoes well, wrap in aluminum foil, and either place directly on the coals in the grill or bake in a pre-heated oven at 480°F (250°C) approx. 60 minutes. Wash and clean the beans, cook in well-salted boiling water for about 10 minutes, and then allow to drain well in a sieve. Wash the thyme, shake dry, and finely chop the leaves. Peel and finely chop the onion. Heat the olive oil in a skillet and sauté the onions for 3 minutes. Add the beans and sauté for 4 more minutes. Stir in the thyme and season with sea salt and pepper.

AH! "Traditional dishes like tzatziki also turn out great using only plantbased products. I buy my soy yogurt in organic grocery stores as they have a large selection. Bon appetit! Or as they say in Greece, kali oreksi!"

Red Fried
POTATOES

INGREDIENTS for 2 portions:

1¾ pounds cooked and peeled
potatoes (800 grams) (from the previous day)

2 white onions

1 garlic clove

8 sun-dried tomatoes without oil

6 tablespoons olive oil

½ cup pine nuts (60 g)

4 tablespoons tomato paste (60 g)

2 teaspoons agave syrup

Sea salt

Freshly ground black pepper

½ bunch fresh basil

PREPARATION TIME: 20 minutes

Cut the cold potatoes into slices that are ⅛ to
¼ inch thick (3–5 mm). Peel and slice both the
onions and garlic. Cut the dried tomatoes into
fine strips. Heat the olive oil in a large skillet and
fry the potatoes over high heat for 4 minutes.
Then turn the potatoes and fry for an additional
4 minutes. Add the onions, garlic, sun-dried
tomatoes, and pine nuts and cook for 2 minutes.
Then add the tomato paste and agave syrup
and fry for 1 minute. Salt and pepper. Stir, making
sure that the tomato paste is mixed in well. In
the meantime, wash, shake dry, and finely chop
the basil. Sprinkle on top of the fried potatoes
and serve.

AH! "When I use potatoes that I cooked
the night before, I don't like to put them
in the fridge overnight because they
tend to have a strange taste the next
day. Instead, I prefer to let them sit out
at room temperature. Of course, you can
also use freshly cooked potatoes, but
don't forget to add in the time it will
take for them to cool down because
peeling hot potatoes isn't much fun."

Red and Green
POTATO LATKES
with Paprika Dip

INGREDIENTS for 4 servings

Paprika Dip:

1¾ cups plain soy yogurt (400 g)

1 red bell pepper

1 teaspoon paprika

2 tablespoons olive oil

Sea salt

Freshly ground black pepper

Potato Latkes:

2¼ pounds waxy potatoes (1 kg)

3 teaspoons potato flour

Sea salt

Freshly ground white pepper

1 red onion

1 white onion

¼ cup sun-dried tomatoes without oil (30 g)

½ bunch basil
(or you can use flat-leaf parsley)

Canola oil

PREPARATION TIME: 35 minutes

For the dip, whip the soy yogurt with a whisk until it's creamy. Wash, clean, and finely chop the bell pepper. Stir the paprika and the rest of the ingredients for the dip into the soy yogurt. Season with sea salt and pepper. For the potato latkes, peel the potatoes and coarsely grate using a kitchen grater. Mix together with the potato flour. Salt and pepper. Halve the red onion and cut into thin slices. Finely chop the white onion and sun-dried tomatoes. Wash the basil, spin dry, and finely chop. Divide the potato mixture in half. For the red latkes, mix in the sun-dried tomatoes and red onion. For the green latkes, fold in the white onion and basil. Heat the canola oil in a skillet. For each latke, place a tablespoon of the mixture in the oil, press down, and fry on each side for about 5 minutes.

AH! "It's best to transfer the latkes to a plate lined with paper towels to drain. Then they'll be lighter and a bit crisper."

VEGETABLE PIZZA
with Pesto

VEGETABLE PIZZA
with Pesto

INGREDIENTS for 2 pizzas

Pizza Dough:

½ cube fresh yeast or 1 package
dry yeast

1 teaspoon raw cane sugar

2 cups all-purpose flour (250 g)

¾–1 teaspoon sea salt

Tomato Sauce:

½ bunch oregano

½ bunch basil

½ cup tomato purée (125 mL)

Sea salt

Freshly ground black pepper

Toppings:

½ zucchini

½ eggplant

½ cup canned corn (70 g)

2 tablespoons olive oil

2 cups arugula (50 g)

Pine Nut Topping:

1 tablespoon pine nuts

1 tablespoon nutritional yeast
flakes

Sea salt

Tomato Pesto:

4 sun-dried tomatoes

3½ tablespoons olive oil (50 mL)

AH! "Eggplants are often somewhat bitter.
If you drizzle a little olive oil on top and
sprinkle liberally with salt after cutting the
eggplants, the bitterness will disappear.
After an hour, rinse the salt off and prepare
as described. I recommend baking the
pizzas one after the other."

PREPARATION TIME:

40 minutes plus approx. 40 minutes rising
time and 10 minutes bake time

For the dough, combine the yeast with just
over ½ cup (125 mL) lukewarm water, raw
cane sugar, and 2 tablespoons flour, and
allow to sit for 10 minutes. Then add the sea
salt and about ⅔ of the remaining flour and
knead well with a hand mixer or by hand.
Gradually add the rest of the flour until the
dough no longer sticks to the side of the
bowl. Depending on the brand of flour you
are using and the climate where you live, the
ratio of water to flour might vary a bit. If the
dough is too firm or doesn't stick together,
add a bit of water. If it is too moist, then add
a little flour. The dough is just right when it
feels elastic and a little moist, but doesn't stick
to your fingers. Place in a bowl and cover with
a greased piece of plastic wrap. Then allow
to rise in a warm spot approx. 20–40 minutes
until the dough is visibly larger. It's best if it
doubles its size. In the meantime, wash the
herbs for the tomato sauce, shake dry, finely
chop, and remove any larger stems. Mix with
the tomato purée, and then season with salt
and pepper. Preheat the oven to 480°F (250°C).

For the topping, wash the zucchini and eggplant, and then cut into thin slices. Allow the corn to drain. In a skillet, sauté the vegetables in olive oil for 3 minutes. Wash the arugula and spin dry. Put the pine nuts, nutritional yeast flakes, and 1 pinch of sea salt in a blender and mix. Divide the dough in half and dust with a little oil. On a well-floured work surface, roll the dough out into two round pizza crusts with a rolling pin. Place the crusts on a baking sheet lined with parchment paper. Allow to sit at least 10 minutes under a kitchen towel. Then spread the tomato sauce on the pizzas and top with the vegetables. Bake in the oven on the lowest rung approx. 10 minutes. In the meantime, prepare the pesto by mixing the sun-dried tomatoes and the olive oil well in a blender. If the blender doesn't manage to make a pesto out of the tomatoes, it won't change the taste at all. Take the pizzas out of the oven. Put the arugula on top and drizzle the tomato pesto over everything. If you miss having parmesan on your pizza, you can get a very similar effect with the pine nut mixture. (It enhances the flavor if you toast the pine nuts in a dry skillet.)

PIZZA SPINACI

INGREDIENTS for 2 pizzas

Pizza Dough:

½ cube fresh yeast or 1 package
dry yeast

1 teaspoon raw cane sugar

2 cups all-purpose flour (250 g)

¾ teaspoon sea salt

Cashew Cream:

1 cup cashews (150 g)

1 teaspoon freshly squeezed
lemon juice

Sea salt

Freshly ground black pepper

Tomato Sauce:

Fresh herbs (e.g., oregano and basil)

½ cup tomato purée (125 mL)

Sea salt

Freshly ground black pepper

Toppings:

1 red onion

2⅔ cups baby spinach (80 g)

¼ cup pine nuts (30 g)

Sea salt

3 tablespoons olive oil

AH! "I also recommend baking these pizzas
one after the other. You can bake them for the
first 5 minutes without spinach if you want to
keep the spinach from collapsing too much. The
pizza ends up looking nicer. It also works well to
replace the cashew cream with cashew cheese,
which you can now find in the refrigerated
section of organic grocery stores."

PREPARATION TIME: 30 minutes plus
approx. 40 minutes rising time and
10 minutes bake time

Prepare the dough as for the vegetable pizza on
the previous page. For the cashew cream, purée
the cashews and just over 3 tablespoons (50 mL)
of water with an immersion blender. Stir in the
lemon juice, and then salt and pepper. Preheat
the oven to 480°F (250°C). For the tomato sauce,
wash the herbs, shake dry, and finely chop the
leaves. Mix with the tomato purée, and then
season with salt and pepper. For the toppings,
peel the onion and cut into thin rings. Wash the
baby spinach well and allow to drain. Dust your
work surface with flour and line a baking sheet
with parchment paper. Divide the dough in half,
form into 2 oval crusts, and place these on the
baking sheet. Spread the tomato sauce on top,
and then add the spinach, onions, and pine nuts.
Sprinkle with salt and drizzle olive oil on top. Bake
in the hot oven for about 10 minutes. After baking,
drop spoonfuls of the cashew cream evenly over
the two pizzas. Sprinkle salt and pepper on top.

DON CANNELLONI
with Basil

INGREDIENTS for 4 servings

Filling:

21 ounces tofu (600 g)

2 onions

2 garlic cloves

1 bunch basil

3½ tablespoons olive oil (50 mL)

⅓ cup pine nuts (50 g)

2 level teaspoons sea salt

8 tablespoons soy cream

Freshly ground black pepper

Tomato Sauce:

1⅔ cups tomato purée (400 mL)

1 tablespoon olive oil

1 tablespoon agave syrup

Sea salt

Freshly ground black pepper

Béchamel Sauce:

1 tablespoon vegetable margarine

1 teaspoon all-purpose flour

150 mL soy cream (e.g., Soyatoo!)

Sea salt

Freshly ground black pepper

Cannelloni:

1½ cups and 2 tablespoons
all-purpose flour (200 g)

AH! "Make sure that the tomato sauce covers the cannelloni evenly so that the pasta will cook well. Otherwise, you'll end up with parts that are dry. There's nothing more delicious than homemade pasta, and with a good pasta machine, your pasta will be ready in no time at all."

PREPARATION TIME:

35 minutes plus 30 minutes bake time

Preheat the oven to 400°F (200°C). For the filling, mash the tofu with a fork. Peel and finely chop the onions and garlic. Wash the basil, shake dry, and finely chop. Heat the olive oil in a skillet and fry the tofu over high heat for 8 minutes. Add the onions, garlic, and pine nuts, and sauté for 3 minutes. Then fold in the basil, sea salt, and soy cream and season liberally with pepper. For the tomato sauce, combine the tomato purée, oil, and agave syrup, and season with salt and pepper. For the Béchamel sauce, heat the margarine in a small saucepan. Add the flour and cook for 2 minutes until the flour is incorporated. Stir in the soy cream with a whisk and allow the sauce to thicken. Salt and pepper. For the cannelloni, combine the flour and 6½ tablespoons (100 mL) water and knead until you have a smooth dough. Use a pasta machine to roll the dough out into long pieces. Then cut the dough into rectangles that are the same size as your baking dish. Spread the tofu mixture on the pieces of dough, roll them up and put them into the baking dish so that they are very close to each other. Pour the tomato sauce evenly over the cannelloni and top with the Béchamel sauce. Bake in a hot oven approx. 30 minutes.

PASTA CARBONARA

INGREDIENTS for 2 servings

3.5 ounces smoked tofu (100 g)

8.8 ounces pasta (250 g) (e.g., ribbon noodles)

Sea salt

1 onion

½ bunch fresh flat-leaf parsley

3 tablespoons olive oil

¾–1 cup soy or oat cream (200 mL)

1 tablespoon vegetable margarine

Freshly ground black pepper

PREPARATION TIME: 15 minutes

Cut the smoked tofu into small cubes. Cook the noodles according to the package instructions in an ample amount of well-salted boiling water until the noodles are al dente. Then allow them to drain in a sieve. Peel and finely dice the onion. Wash the parsley, spin dry, and finely chop. Fry the tofu cubes in hot olive oil until they are a little crispy. Add the diced onions and sauté for 3 minutes. Deglaze with the soy cream, margarine, and ⅔ of the parsley. Salt and pepper. Mix the carbonara with the pasta. Sprinkle freshly ground pepper and the rest of the chopped parsley on top. Serve.

AH! "It's really important to use a high-quality, neutral margarine for this recipe. You can find non-hydrogenated margarine in organic grocery stores that have a very neutral taste and sometimes even taste a bit like butter. If you don't have any neutral tasting margarine at home, then use olive oil instead. Freshly ground pepper is also absolutely essential for this recipe—please avoid buying the pre-ground pepper sold at the supermarket—that'll mess up the recipe!"

TAGLIATELLE
with Asparagus in a Saffron Orange Cream

INGREDIENTS for 2 servings

½ medium-size bunch of
asparagus (250 g)

7 ounces tagliatelle (200 g)

Sea salt

1 red onion

2 tablespoons olive oil

½ organic orange

6½ tablespoons white almond
butter (100 g)

½ teaspoon saffron threads

¼ cup sun-dried tomatoes without
oil (30 g)

PREPARATION TIME: 45 minutes

Wash the asparagus. Peel the lower third of
the asparagus spears and cut off the woody
ends. Cut diagonally into approx. 1 inch (2.5 cm)
pieces. Cook the tagliatelle according to the
package instructions in well-salted water until
the noodles are al dente. Cook the asparagus in
a saucepan for 8–10 minutes, drain, and set to
the side. Peel and halve the onion. Cut into thin
slices and sauté in hot olive oil for 3 minutes.
Grate half of the orange peel and squeeze
the juice from the orange. Whisk together the
almond butter and just over ½ cup (130 mL)
cold water. Add this mixture, the orange juice,
and the grated orange peel to the onions. Add
the asparagus and tagliatelle. Season with sea
salt and saffron. Cut the sun-dried tomatoes in
fine strips to use as garnish.

AH! "Saffron is very fragrant and is
known to be the most expensive spice
in the world: a small package costs
about 12 dollars at an organic grocery
store. Orange peel contains a lot of
substances that can protect our body
from cancer—but its main function
here is to make this dish fragrant."

RED PASTA
with Mushroom Cream Sauce

INGREDIENTS for 2 servings

Pasta:

1⅔ cups all-purpose flour (200 g)

⅓–½ cup beet juice (100 mL)

Sea salt

1 tablespoon olive oil

Mushroom Cream Sauce:

1 onion

About 12 brown mushrooms (250 g)

½ bunch fresh oregano

6½ tablespoons white almond
butter (100 g)

2 tablespoons olive oil

Sea salt

Freshly ground black pepper

AH! "I really recommend purchasing
a high-quality pasta machine. With
this machine, you'll be a 'pasta pro'
in no time. And your friends will be
amazed by your fantastic spaghetti,
tagliatelle, and linguine. But don't do
what I did: never clean your pasta
machine with water! I did that once
and the machine rusted."

PREPARATION TIME: 45 minutes

For the pasta, knead the flour and beet juice
together. Roll out the dough into a long sheet
and dust it with flour. Then run the dough
through a pasta machine a few times (up to
Setting 5). With a sharp knife, cut the sheets
of pasta dough lengthwise into wide ribbon
noodles that are about ¾ of an inch (2 cm) wide.
Cook the pasta for 2 minutes in well-salted
boiling water. Carefully pour into a sieve and
allow to drain. Then pour back into the saucepan
and toss with a little olive oil.

For the mushroom cream sauce, peel and finely
chop the onion. Clean and finely slice the
mushrooms. Wash the oregano, shake dry, and
pluck the leaves off. Mix the almond butter
with approx. ½ cup (130 mL) water and whisk
together until smooth. Heat the olive oil in a
skillet and sauté the onions for 2 minutes. Then
add the mushrooms and sauté for an additional
3 minutes. Add the almond butter, remove from
heat, add the oregano, and season to taste with
salt and pepper. Put the noodles on plates and
pour the mushroom cream sauce on top.

POTATOES AND PORCINI MUSHROOM RAVIOLI

in Broccoli Cream Sauce

INGREDIENTS for 2–3 servings

Filling:

2 medium-size starchy potatoes (400 g)

Sea salt

½ bunch flat-leaf parsley

5–6 porcini mushrooms (100 g)
(or another type of mushroom in season)

Olive oil

Freshly ground black pepper

Ravioli:

1⅔ cups all-purpose flour (200 g)

Cream Sauce:

3½ –4 cups broccoli florets (250–300 g)

Sea salt

1 onion

1 tablespoon olive oil

1 cup oat cream (250 mL)
(or soy cream, e.g., Soyatoo!)

Freshly grated nutmeg

Freshly ground black pepper

AH! "The cooking time for the broccoli florets will vary, depending on how large they are. Try to cut them all about the same size and test them every once and a while to see if they are done. I don't like broccoli at all when it is overcooked. So, be careful. Broccoli should always be crisp-tender."

PREPARATION TIME: 60 minutes

For the filling, peel and coarsely chop the potatoes. Then cook them in well-salted water for 12 minutes until they are soft. Pour into a sieve and allow to cool for 5 minutes. Then place the potatoes in a saucepan and mash with a potato masher. Wash the parsley, shake dry, and finely chop the leaves. Clean and wash the porcini mushrooms and allow to drain on a couple of paper towels. Then finely chop the mushrooms and sauté in hot olive oil in a skillet for 3 minutes. Add the mushrooms and parsley to the potatoes, mix well, and season liberally with sea salt and pepper. For the ravioli, combine the flour and 6½ tablespoons (100 mL) water and then knead until the dough is smooth. Form the dough into a rectangle and dust with flour. Run through a pasta machine (up to Setting 5) several times until the 2 sheets of dough are each about 20 x 6 inches (50 x 15 cm). Place one of the sheets of dough on a well-floured work surface. Spoon the potato mixture with a teaspoon onto the dough so that you have two rows and the spoonfuls are about an inch (2–3 cm) apart. Lay the second sheet of dough right over the top and cut the ravioli out with a ravioli wheel. Press the dough together on the sides a little with your fingers so that air bubbles won't form when the ravioli cook. For the cream sauce, wash the broccoli, cut into small florets, and boil in well-salted water for 3 minutes. Peel and finely chop the onion. Heat the olive oil in a skillet and sauté the onions over high heat for 2 minutes. Deglaze with the oat cream, cook for 1 minute longer, and then season with nutmeg, salt, and pepper. Carefully fold in the broccoli. Allow the ravioli to cook until done in an ample amount of well-salted boiling water for 5 minutes. The ravioli is done when it floats up to the top. Remove the ravioli from the pan with a slotted spoon and allow to drain for a short while. Serve the ravioli on plates with the broccoli cream sauce.

GOULASH

INGREDIENTS for 2 servings

5.5 ounces textured soy protein
(chunks or strips) (150 g)

Sea salt

½ cup vegetable oil (110 mL)

2 onions

2 red bell peppers

½ red chili pepper

2 garlic cloves

4 teaspoons sweet paprika

½ teaspoon dried marjoram

Ground caraway

1 tablespoon tomato paste

6½ tablespoons red wine (100 mL)

Grated peel of ½ organic lemon

1½ tablespoons agave syrup

3 tablespoons oat or soy cream

1 small loaf of rye bread

AH! "Dry soy chunks or strips are sometimes called textured soy protein. This product is the result of an elaborate process, in which soy beans take on a meat-like texture. Dry soy is available in a variety of forms: cubes, cutlets, nuggets, ground, or, like here, as chunks or strips. For vegetarians who like dishes that have a meaty texture, these are great for when you're hungry for something really hearty! But, do buy these products in organic grocery stores since they pay special attention to the quality of their soy products."

PREPARATION TIME: 45 minutes

Soak the textured soy protein in hot, well-salted water for 10 minutes. Then press the water out and fry in a non-stick skillet in ¼ cup (60 mL) vegetable oil over high heat approx. 8 minutes. In the meantime, peel the onions and cut into thin rings. Wash the bell peppers, remove the seeds, and cut into strips. Remove the seeds from the chili pepper and finely chop. Peel and finely chop the garlic. Remove the textured soy protein from the skillet and set aside. Sauté the onions and bell peppers in 3 tablespoons (50 mL) vegetable oil for 5 minutes. Add the garlic and chili pepper and cook for 2 minutes. Add the textured soy protein, paprika, marjoram, and 2 pinches caraway, and sauté for 3 more minutes. Add the tomato paste and cook for 2 minutes. Add the red wine, 1¼ cups (300 mL) water, lemon peel, salt, and agave syrup, and cook everything for 5 minutes until the mixture is creamy. Finally, add the oat or soy cream and allow to cool for 5 minutes. Cut off the top of a small loaf of rye bread. Scoop out the inside and serve the goulash in the bread.

LEEK QUICHE

INGREDIENTS for 4 servings in 1 quiche pan (Diameter: 9½ inches or 24 cm)

1⅔ cups flour (200 g)

1¾ cups whole wheat flour (200 g)

2 teaspoons baking powder

Sea salt

1 cup vegetable margarine (220 g)

2 tablespoons raw cane sugar

2–3 leeks

3.5 ounces smoked tofu (100 g)

3½ tablespoons olive oil (50 mL)

1 red chili pepper

2 cups soy or oat cream (500 mL)

4½ tablespoons cornstarch (40 g)

Freshly ground black pepper

PREPARATION TIME:

30 minutes plus 40 minutes bake time

Preheat the oven to 350°F (180°C). Combine the flour and whole wheat flour with the baking powder, 2 teaspoons sea salt, margarine, raw cane sugar, and 4½ tablespoons (70 mL) cold water, and knead until you have a crumbly dough. Clean and wash the leek, and then cut into fine rings. Cut the smoked tofu into small cubes and fry in hot olive oil for 5 minutes. Add the leeks and sauté for 2 minutes. Wash the chili pepper, remove the seeds, and finely chop. Combine the soy or oat cream with the cornstarch, add the chili pepper, and season liberally with salt and pepper. Stir the tofu and leeks into the cream mixture. Roll the dough into a circle (diameter approx. 10 inches or 25 cm), line the quiche pan with the dough, and press the dough up on the sides. Pour in the leek mixture. Bake for 40 minutes and then allow to cool so that the quiche can set. Serve lukewarm.

AH! "This is a hearty quiche made with healthy leeks. Leeks are rich in Vitamins C and K and also contain a lot of folic acid, potassium, manganese, magnesium, and iron."

NASI GORENG

INGREDIENTS for 2 servings

¾ cup fresh peas (80 g)

Sea salt

3 tablespoons cashews (30 g)

6 tablespoons canola oil

3⅓ cups cooked Basmati rice (400 g)
(from the previous day)

½ teaspoon curry powder

½ red bell pepper

½ yellow chili pepper

1 medium-size red onion

3 ounces seitan (80 g)

1 tablespoon soy sauce

PREPARATION TIME: 25 minutes

Cook the peas in well-salted boiling water approx. 5 minutes. Toast the cashews in a dry skillet and then remove from the skillet. Heat 3 tablespoons canola oil in a skillet and fry the rice over high heat for 7 minutes. Sprinkle the curry powder on top, stir well, and then remove everything from the skillet. Wash the bell pepper and chili pepper, remove the seeds, and cut into thin strips. Peel the onion, cut in half, and then slice. Cut the seitan into strips, fry in 2 tablespoons of hot canola oil for 3 minutes, remove from the skillet, and transfer to a plate lined with paper towels to drain. Put the bell pepper, chili pepper, onions and peas in the skillet with 1 tablespoon canola oil and sauté approx. 3 minutes. Add the rice and seitan, and season with soy sauce and salt. Serve in bowls and garnish with cashews.

AH! "Cashews aren't only an excellent source of the amino acid tryptophan, but they also contain a lot of copper and magnesium. I recommend having a cup of hot, organic green tea with this dish. You'll feel a little like you were in Asia."

CRESCENT MOON SATAYS
with Stir-Fried Vegetables

INGREDIENTS for 2 servings

Satay Sauce:

2 garlic cloves

1 red chili pepper

1 tablespoon olive oil

6½ tablespoons peanut butter (100 g)

1¼ cups unsweetened coconut milk (150 mL)

1 tablespoon soy sauce

1 tablespoon agave syrup

1 tablespoon freshly squeezed

lemon juice

Wok Vegetables:

9 ounces rice noodles (250 g)

Sea salt

1 small carrot

½ red bell pepper

½ yellow bell pepper

½ cup Chinese cabbage (50 g)

½ zucchini

1 scallion

3 tablespoons sesame oil

3 tablespoons soy sauce

Crescent Moon Satay:

7 ounces tempeh (200 g)

3 tablespoons canola oil

2 tablespoons soy sauce

Sea salt

2 wooden skewers

Crescent moon cookie cutters (or another shape)

In addition:

3 tablespoons peanuts (30 g)

½ chili pepper

¼ bunch cilantro leaves

PREPARATION TIME: 45 minutes

For the sauce, peel and finely chop the garlic. Wash the chili pepper, remove the seeds, and finely chop. Heat the olive oil in a saucepan, and sauté the chili pepper and garlic for 1 minute. Add the rest of the ingredients for the sauce, stir, and then set aside. For the wok vegetables, cook the rice noodles in well-salted boiling water according to the package instructions until al dente. Peel the carrot and cut diagonally into fine slices. Wash and clean the other vegetables. Remove the seeds from the bell peppers. Cut the Chinese cabbage and bell peppers into thin strips. Cut the zucchini into thin slices and the scallions into thin rings. Heat the sesame oil in a wok or a skillet and sauté the vegetables over high heat approx. 4 minutes. Add the rice noodles and soy sauce and cook for 3 more minutes. For the crescent moon satays, cut crescent moons out of the tempeh. Heat the canola oil in a skillet and fry the tempeh 3 minutes on each side over high heat. Season with soy sauce and sea salt. Stick the crescent moons on the 2 wooden skewers. Coarsely chop the peanuts. Wash the chili pepper, remove the seeds, and cut into strips. Wash the cilantro, shake dry, and finely chop. Mix the peanuts, chili pepper, and cilantro together. On plates, arrange the wok vegetables with the skewers and sauce. Sprinkle the cilantro nut mixture on top and serve.

AH! "Tempeh is made from fermented soybeans and tastes a bit nutty—it takes a little getting used to. But I now love both the texture and the taste. You can get tempeh at an organic grocery store."

CREPE ROLLS
with a Mushroom and Walnut Filling

INGREDIENTS for 2 servings

10 porcini mushrooms (230 g)
(alternatively, brown mushrooms or king oyster mushrooms)

2 red onions

1 garlic clove

9 tablespoons olive oil

1 cup walnuts (130 g)

Sea salt

Freshly ground black pepper

⅔ cup first clear flour (85 g)
(If not available, you can use bread flour.)

⅔ cup unsweetened soy milk (160 mL)

Canola oil

3 vine-ripened tomatoes

1 orange bell pepper

Living watercress

AH! "Crepes are quite a bit thinner than pancakes. You can buy special crepe pans and batter spreaders, which I strongly recommend. If you don't have these, you can use the bottom of a ladle and rotate the pan so that the batter gets distributed evenly. But do make the crepes paper thin; otherwise, the rolls will turn out too big."

PREPARATION TIME: 30 minutes

For the filling, clean the porcini mushrooms, and if necessary, wash them. Finely chop the mushrooms. Peel and finely dice the onions and garlic. Heat 5 tablespoons olive oil in a skillet and sauté the onions for 2 minutes. Add the garlic and mushrooms and sauté approx. 5 minutes while stirring. Finely chop the walnuts, stir them into the mushroom mixture, and liberally season with salt and pepper. For the crepe batter, combine the flour, soy milk, and 1 pinch of sea salt. Lightly brush a non-stick pan with canola oil. Pour the batter into the pan with a ladle, and then spread it out evenly using the bottom of the ladle. Cook on each side approx. 2 minutes, until the crepe is golden brown. Repeat this process to make 4 paper-thin crepes. For the sauce, wash and clean the vine-ripened tomatoes, and then purée them with an immersion blender. Wash the bell pepper, remove the seeds, and finely dice. Sauté the bell pepper in 2 tablespoons hot olive oil for 3 minutes. Add the puréed tomatoes and 2 tablespoons olive oil, and season with salt and pepper. Fill the crepes with the Mushroom Walnut Mixture, roll them up, and cut into pieces at an angle. Serve on plates with the tomato sauce and garnish with watercress.

TOFU
with an Herb Crust and Duchess Potatoes

INGREDIENTS for 2 servings

2 medium-size starchy potatoes (400 g)

Sea salt

2½ cups green cabbage (250 g)

6 tablespoons canola oil

6½ tablespoons almond butter (100 g)

Freshly ground black pepper

½ bunch flat-leaf parsley

1 sprig of rosemary

2 slices of multigrain bread

4½ tablespoons olive oil (70 mL)

7 ounces tofu (200 g)

2 tablespoons vegetable margarine

Freshly grated nutmeg

2 tablespoons toasted pine nuts

Cranberry preserves

AH! "Tofu can also be festive! This is a version with a hearty herb crust that is nicely seasoned—a great holiday meal."

PREPARATION TIME: 45 minutes

Cook the potatoes in well-salted boiling water approx. 30 minutes. In the meantime, cut the pointed cabbage into thin strips. Heat 3 tablespoons canola oil in a skillet and sauté the cabbage for 5 minutes. Combine the almond butter with ½ cup (120 mL) water, and add this mixture to the cabbage. Reduce the heat and season the cabbage with sea salt and pepper. Wash the herbs and spin dry. Chop the herbs and bread and purée in a blender together with about 3½ tablespoons (50 mL) olive oil. Salt and pepper liberally. Preheat the oven to 400°F (200°C). Cut the tofu into slices that are just under ½ inch (1 cm). Heat 3 tablespoons canola oil in a skillet and fry the tofu slices 5 minutes on each side. Spread the herb mixture on the tofu slices, press the two layers together, and place on a baking sheet. Peel the potatoes and mash with a potato masher. Mix with the margarine, and season with nutmeg and sea salt. Put the potato mixture into a pastry bag, and then pipe rosettes that are the size of walnuts onto a greased baking sheet. Bake both the tofu slices and potatoes in a hot oven for about 10 minutes. The duchess potatoes are done when they're golden brown. Serve the duchess potatoes with the tofu, cabbage, toasted pine nuts, and some cranberry preserves.

This chapter is dedicated to all of you who are party people. You simply have to celebrate the special events as they come. And as a vegan, you'll also want to offer your guests something. Although I'm not what you would call a missionary, I think special events are a great opportunity to improve the image that vegan food has.

Experience has shown me that guests not only love finger foods and delicious noodle and pasta salads, but also mini pizzas. For the pizzas, you can make the dough, roll it out, and stack the crusts in the fridge between pieces of parchment paper. Your friends can then top their pizzas as they like. Instead of cheese, you can use cashew cream, pine nut parmesan, or pesto—delicious, juicy, and totally without cheese that is packed with cholesterol!

For those with a sweet tooth, the best choices are tiramisu or a large bowl of chocolate mousse. Then everyone will have something they like. Both of these are so popular that when guests come late, they are often out of luck and everything's already gone.

And, yes, I also love barbecuing with friends. Some of my friends eat meat and others are vegetarians. I've made it a habit to respect every person as they are. I always make salads and dips in advance, get the grill going at the beginning of the party, throw an apron on, and arm myself with BBQ tongs and an aluminum bowl. Then I barbecue mushrooms with an herb filling, kabobs with crisp vegetables and smoked tofu, vegan hamburgers and chicken wings, BBQ tofu, sesame flat bread, or teriyaki eggplants. And then the grand finale comes—grilled caramelized bananas with chocolate sauce and vegan marshmallows. Some things are so simple, but yet so delicious! So, let the barbecue season begin—and luckily there are parties at friends' houses all year long!

VEGGIE PARTY

STUFFED TOMATOES
with a Yogurt Nut Cream

INGREDIENTS for 2 servings

6 medium vine-ripened tomatoes
(try to find a variety of colors)

½ cup cashews (70 g)

⅔ cup soy yogurt (150 g)

5 sun-dried tomatoes without oil
(25 g)

1 tablespoon chopped oregano
leaves

1 tablespoon chopped basil leaves

Sea salt

Freshly ground black pepper

PREPARATION TIME: 25 minutes

Cut the tops off of the vine-ripened tomatoes so that they each have a lid. Carefully scoop out the inside of each tomato with a teaspoon—you can use this for other purposes. Finely grind the cashews in a blender and mix with the soy yogurt. Finely chop the sun-dried tomatoes. Combine the sun-dried tomatoes, and the chopped oregano and basil leaves with the yogurt nut mixture. Season with salt and pepper. Fill the tomatoes with this mixture.

AH! "Cashews are very rich in tryptophan, an essential amino acid. Our body uses this amino acid to produce serotonin, which makes us feel happy."

POTATO SALAD

INGREDIENTS for 4 servings

3–3½ pounds medium-size waxy potatoes (1.5 kg)

Sea salt

2 red onions

½ bunch dill

½ bunch flat-leaf parsley

1 large bunch radishes (200 g)

6½ tablespoons canola oil (100 mL)

2 tablespoons white wine vinegar

1 cup unsweetened oat milk (250 mL)

1½ teaspoons locust bean gum
(If not available, you can use guar gum.)

Freshly ground white pepper

2 cups pickles (300 g)

PREPARATION TIME:

40 minutes plus 2 hours wait time

Boil the potatoes in well-salted water approx. 25 minutes. They should still be a bit firm. Peel them while still hot, cut into slices, and allow to cool. In the meantime, peel the onions, cut them in half, and finely slice into rings. Wash and finely chop the dill and parsley. Wash and clean the radishes and cut into fine slices. Whip the canola oil, white wine vinegar, oat milk, and locust bean gum with an immersion blender for about 3 minutes until the mayonnaise is smooth. Season with sea salt and white pepper. Cut the pickles into fine slices. Carefully mix all ingredients in a bowl and let sit for approx. 2 hours to allow the flavors to meld.

AH! "Vegan mayo is really very creamy and easy to make. And you don't need very many ingredients. You should always make a fresh batch and avoid storing it in the refrigerator for too long because then it won't taste as good."

TORTILLA CHIPS
with Avocado Cream and Hot Salsa

INGREDIENTS for 2 servings

Chips:

¾ cup and 2 tablespoons corn flour (100 g)

1 teaspoon sea salt

1 tablespoon olive oil

1 teaspoon paprika

Salsa:

1 onion

½ red bell pepper

¼ chili pepper

½ pint cherry tomatoes (150 g)

¼ bunch cilantro

2 tablespoons olive oil

2 tablespoons tomato paste

1 tablespoon agave syrup

Juice from ½ lemon

Sea salt

Freshly ground black pepper

Avocado Cream:

1 avocado

1 teaspoon freshly squeezed lemon juice

Sea salt

Freshly ground black pepper

AH! "For this recipe, it's really important to roll the dough out paper thin and to brush it with a thin layer of oil. If you do it correctly, you'll have some of the oil paprika mixture left over."

PREPARATION TIME: 30 minutes plus 10 minutes bake time and 30 minutes cooling time

Preheat the oven to 350°F (180°C). Combine the corn flour, just over ⅔ cup (165 mL) hot boiling water, and ½ teaspoon sea salt, and allow to sit for a short while until it has thickened a bit. First, stir with a fork and then knead to a smooth dough with your hands (as you would do for pastry crust). With a rolling pin, roll the dough out between two sheets of parchment paper until it is paper thin! Remove the top sheet of parchment paper and carefully transfer the dough and the bottom sheet of parchment paper to a baking sheet. Combine the olive oil with ½ teaspoon sea salt and paprika, and brush a thin layer of this mixture on the dough. Bake in the middle of a hot oven for 10 minutes, allow to cool for 30 minutes, and then cut into triangles with a sharp knife. For the salsa, peel and finely chop the onion. Wash and remove the seeds from both the bell pepper and chili pepper. Cut the paprika into cubes and the chili pepper into fine strips. Wash the cherry tomatoes and cut them into quarters. Wash the cilantro, spin dry, and finely chop the leaves. Heat the olive oil in a small saucepan. Sauté the onions, paprika, and chili for 4 minutes. Fold in the tomato paste and agave syrup and allow to caramelize for 1 minute. Add the cherry tomatoes and cook for 3 more minutes. Fold in the cilantro and lemon juice, and then season with salt and pepper. For the avocado cream, halve and peel the avocado and then remove the pit. Purée the avocado with the lemon juice in a blender. Season with salt and pepper. Serve the tortilla chips with the salsa and avocado cream.

CRISPY TOFU NUGGETS
with Homemade Curry Ketchup

INGREDIENTS for 2 servings

Tofu Nuggets:

½ cup all-purpose flour (65 g)

1 teaspoon raw cane sugar

1 teaspoon sea salt

2¾ cups unsweetened cornflakes (100 g)

14 ounces tofu (400 g)

2 cups vegetable oil (500 mL)

Curry Ketchup:

Juice from ½ lemon

⅔ cup tomato paste (140 g)

2 tablespoons agave syrup

1 teaspoon curry powder

2 tablespoons olive oil

Sea salt

Freshly ground black pepper

PREPARATION TIME: 25 minutes

For the nuggets, stir the flour together with the raw cane sugar, sea salt, and 6 tablespoons (90 mL) water until the batter is smooth. Finely crumble the cornflakes. Cut the tofu into slices that are just under ½ inch (1 cm), and then use a knife to shape the tofu into nuggets. Dip the nuggets in the batter and then coat them with the cornflakes. Heat the vegetable oil in a deep fryer or a small saucepan. You'll know the oil is hot enough if you dip a wooden toothpick into the oil and small bubbles float up to the top around the toothpick. Fry the nuggets approx. 3 minutes. Transfer to a plate lined with paper towels to drain. For the curry ketchup, mix all of the ingredients with 3 tablespoons water. Serve with the nuggets.

AH! "If you don't want to deep fry the nuggets, you can also fry them in a skillet. Just fry them on all sides in ⅓ cup (80 mL) vegetable oil until they are golden brown."

OLIVE AND TOMATO
FOCACCIA BREAD
with Eggplant Dip

INGREDIENTS for 2 servings

Focaccia Bread:

½ cube fresh yeast or 1 pkg. yeast

1 teaspoon raw cane sugar

2 cups first clear flour (250 g)
(If not available, you can use bread flour.)

1½ teaspoons sea salt

1 rosemary sprig

4 sun-dried tomatoes without oil

3 garlic cloves

½ cup pitted green olives (50 g)

½ cup pitted black olives (50 g)

1 tablespoon olive oil

Coarse sea salt

Eggplant Dip:

1 large eggplant (500 g)

1 small onion

3 garlic cloves

4 tablespoons olive oil

½ bunch basil

1 teaspoon sea salt

Freshly ground black pepper

2 teaspoons freshly squeezed
lemon juice

AH! "Poke holes in the eggplant to prevent it from exploding in the oven, which happened to me once."

PREPARATION TIME FOCACCIA: 20 minutes plus 40 minutes rising time and 35 minutes bake time
Combine the yeast, raw cane sugar, and 3 rounded tablespoons flour with just over ½ cup (125 mL) warm water. Allow to rest for 10 minutes. Add the sea salt and the remaining flour and knead until the dough is smooth. If necessary, add a little warm water. The dough should be moist, but shouldn't stick to your fingers. Allow to rise covered in a warm spot for about 30 minutes. Preheat the oven to 350°F (180°C). Wash the rosemary, shake dry, pluck off the leaves, and coarsely chop. Cut the sun-dried tomatoes into strips. Peel the garlic and thinly slice. Dust your work surface with plenty of flour. Line a baking sheet with parchment paper. Shape the dough into a rectangle with rounded corners that is about 1 inch (2½ cm) thick. Use your finger to press evenly spaced dimples into the dough that are almost as deep as the dough. Bake in a hot oven on a baking sheet for about 35 minutes. Toss the garlic slices and the sun-dried tomato strips with 1 tablespoon oil. About 5 minutes before the end of the bake time, top the focaccia bread with the garlic, sun-dried tomatoes, rosemary, and olives, pressing lightly into the crust. Sprinkle with the coarse sea salt.

PREPARATION TIME FOR THE DIP: 60 minutes
Preheat the oven to 350°F (180°C). Poke holes into all sides of the eggplant, and then place it on a baking sheet lined with parchment paper. Bake in a hot oven for about 45 minutes and then let cool. Cut the eggplant in half lengthwise, and scoop out the eggplant flesh. Peel and finely chop both the onion and garlic. Heat the oil in a skillet, and sauté the onion and garlic for about 4 minutes. Wash the basil, shake dry, and pluck off the leaves. Purée all ingredients in a blender, and season with sea salt, pepper, and lemon juice.

VEGGIE SHISH KEBABS
with Basil Dip and Spicy Salsa

INGREDIENTS for 4 kebabs
(2 servings)

Shish Kebabs:

½ bell pepper

½ zucchini

¼ eggplant

4 small mushrooms

4 cherry tomatoes

4 small red onions

3.5 ounces smoked tofu (100 g)

3 tablespoons olive oil

½ teaspoon sweet paprika

Sea salt

4 wooden skewers

Basil Dip:

⅓ cup blanched almonds (50 g)

1 bunch basil

1 garlic clove

6½ tablespoons olive oil (100 mL)

½ teaspoon sea salt

5 pitted black olives

1 tablespoon freshly squeezed
lemon juice

Salsa:

2 red onions

4 garlic cloves

1 thumb-size piece of ginger

½ red bell pepper

2 tablespoons olive oil

½ red chili pepper (a little under 1 inch or 2 cm)

2 rounded teaspoons tomato paste

1 tablespoon agave syrup

2 vine-ripened tomato

4 tablespoons soy sauce

1 pinch cinnamon

Sea salt

Freshly ground black pepper

PREPARATION TIME: 45 minutes

For the shish kebabs, wash and clean the vegetables, peel the onions, and remove the seeds from the bell pepper. Cut the vegetables and the smoked tofu into pieces that are about the same size so that all ingredients will cook evenly on the skewers. Alternately thread the tofu and vegetables onto the skewers. Combine the olive oil with the paprika and a little sea salt. Coat the vegetables and tofu with this mixture and cook on each side for about 8 minutes over medium heat on the grill or in a grill pan. For the basil dip, toast the almonds in a dry skillet for about 1 minute. Wash the basil, shake dry, and pluck off the leaves. Peel the garlic and purée with the other ingredients for the dip in a blender. For the salsa, peel the onions, garlic, and ginger. Wash the bell pepper and chili pepper, and remove the seeds from both. Finely chop the onions, garlic, ginger, bell pepper, and chili pepper. Heat the olive oil in a skillet and sauté the onions, garlic, ginger, and bell pepper for 3 minutes. Add the tomato paste and the agave syrup, stir, and allow to caramelize for 1 minute. Wash and finely chop the vine-ripened tomatoes. Add the tomatoes, the remaining ingredients, and 2 tablespoons water to the skillet, cook for 2 minutes, and season with salt and pepper. Serve the shish kebabs with salsa and dip.

AH! "If you make the salsa and pesto ahead of time, it'll be a lot easier. It's best to grill the kebabs over medium heat; otherwise, they'll get dark too quickly. The edge of the grill works well for this. The combination of salsa that has an Asian touch and Mediterranean basil dip is unusual, but it tastes really good! You can vary the amount of chili pepper you use to make the salsa as spicy as you like."

CHILI
with Avocado Cream

INGREDIENTS for 2 servings

Chili:

2¾ cups canned kidney beans (170 g)

1 cup canned corn (130 g)

7 ounces tofu (200 g)

2 onions

3½ tablespoons olive oil (50 mL)

¾ cup tomato paste (200 g)

3 tablespoons agave syrup

1⅓ cups tomato purée (330 mL)

1 tablespoon dried oregano

½ teaspoon cumin

½ teaspoon chili powder

Freshly ground black pepper

Sea salt

Avocado Cream:

1 avocado

1–1¼ cups soy yogurt (250 g)

Peel and juice from ½ organic
lemon

Sea salt

Freshly ground black pepper

In addition:

1 scallion

Tortilla chips

PREPARATION TIME: 30 minutes

Rinse off the kidney beans and corn and allow to drain briefly. Crumble the tofu with a fork. Peel and coarsely chop the onions. Heat the olive oil in a skillet and fry the tofu approx. 5 minutes. Add the onions and sauté for 5 more minutes. Add the tomato paste and agave syrup and let caramelize briefly. Add the tomato purée, kidney beans, corn, oregano, cumin, chili powder, and pepper, and cook for 2 more minutes. Salt. For the avocado cream, halve the avocado, remove the pit, and scoop the pulp out. Purée the avocado with the soy yogurt. Add the lemon peel and juice; salt and pepper. Wash the scallion and cut into rings. Pour the chili in bowls and top each portion with 2 tablespoons avocado cream. Serve with the tortilla chips and garnish with scallions. Rice or a crispy baguette go well with this dish.

AH! "Chili sin carne works great for parties. Good seasoning is the key to good chili, and you can make it as spicy as you want. For parties, I usually make a big pot that's medium spicy and a small pot for the hardcore—whoever tries some of this will really be testing their limits! That makes the party more fun."

I'm often disappointed by the selection available at our gas stations, snack bars, and convenience stores: baked pizza with imitation cheese (which would actually be vegan), croissants, sandwiches, and coffee! This is the case even though both parties would profit from a healthy variety of foods. Something like my baguette with fragrant parsley pesto, tasty smoked tofu slices, thinly cut strips of carrot, bell pepper, and crisp lettuce. I look forward to the day when I can go to a gas station and say, "Good morning! A vegan pesto baguette please and a matcha latte shake [...] No, not the cashew butter baguette, but the one with pesto and smoked tofu [...] It's right there next to the basil tofu whole grain sandwiches [...] Can I please have the matcha shake, ice cold? Thanks, how much is that altogether?"

Let's be optimistic: it most likely won't be too much longer until this is the case. But some things just don't change overnight. However, the idea is still great: healthy snacks, which give us energy for the day and are both filling and help to keep us slim—and help to protect our environment. Until then, though, we can be content to make great vegan dishes, breads, and desserts at home. My tip for getting everything ready smoothly is to prepare your meals and snacks the evening before. That way, everything will be ready to go even though the next morning is hectic as usual. I recommend looking on the internet for airtight containers, which won't leak at all, not even with homemade soup. For environmental reasons, you should rely on clear plastic wrap rather than aluminum foil since it takes a huge amount of energy to produce aluminum foil. Transparent wrap is not always the best for everything. but it works well to wrap up sandwiches in, and you'll get even more envious looks. Vegan to go for me means: "I'm going to eat well when I'm on the go and do something good for the planet at the same time."

By the way, when you make your own meals, you'll also save a lot of money: A batch of the Best Muesli Bars in Town lasts for a couple of days and is really cheap to make. A large bowl of potato salad is also delicious, healthy, long-lasting, and very inexpensive. However, it would be helpful if each time you're at a convenience store, you would ask for vegan food—otherwise, nothing will ever change.

Vegan TO GO

BEST GRANOLA BARS
in Town

INGREDIENTS

for approx. 24 bars

2¾ cups rolled oats (250 g)

¾ cup chopped hazelnuts (100 g)

1 cup dried bananas (80 g)

1¾ cups cornflakes (60 g)

⅔ cup agave syrup (150 mL)

4 tablespoons soy cream (e.g., Soyatoo!)

½ tablespoon raw cane sugar

2 teaspoons ground vanilla

2 tablespoons flour

Sea salt

7 ounces dark chocolate (200 g)
(50% cocoa)

AH! "When I made some of the recipes for the staff at my publishing company, this recipe was one of everybody's favorites!"

PREPARATION TIME: 20 minutes plus 13 minutes bake time and 30 minutes cooling time

Preheat the oven to 350°F (180°C). While stirring, toast the rolled oats and hazelnuts in a non-stick skillet over medium heat approx. 10 minutes. Coarsely chop the dried bananas and crumble the cornflakes. Mix these ingredients well with the agave syrup, soy cream, raw cane sugar, vanilla, flour, and 2 pinches of sea salt. Spread the mixture out on a baking sheet (approx. 15.5 x 14 inches or 40 x 36 cm) lined with parchment paper so that it is just under ¼ inch (5 mm) thick. Place a second piece of parchment paper that is the same size as the baking sheet on top of the mixture. Use your hands or a rolling pin to smooth the mixture out and press it down so that it will hold together. Bake the mixture with the parchment paper on top in a hot oven approx. 13 minutes. Allow to cool for 30 minutes. Melt the dark chocolate over a hot water bath. To do this, bring some water to a boil in a saucepan and then reduce to medium heat. Allow the chocolate to melt in a metal bowl over the water bath. The metal bowl shouldn't come into contact with the water bath. Cut the mixture into bars that are approx. 4.5 x 2 inches (12 x 5 cm) and dip individually into the melted chocolate. Then place each bar on a sheet of parchment paper to dry.

CASHEW DREAM
Ciabatta

INGREDIENTS for 1 ciabatta (Serves 2)

1 ciabatta baguette

5 tablespoons cashew butter

Sea salt

Freshly ground black pepper

1 cup baby spinach (30 g)

1 avocado

¾ cup red beet sprouts (20 g)
(If not available, you can use other varieties.)

PREPARATION TIME: 15 minutes

Cut the ciabatta open lengthwise and spread the cashew butter on the inside of both halves. Sprinkle with sea salt and pepper. Wash the baby spinach, remove the stems, and spin dry. Peel and halve the avocado and remove the pit. Finely slice the avocado. Wash the red beet sprouts and allow to drain. Layer the bottom half of the ciabatta with the spinach, avocado slices, and sprouts. Place the upper half of the ciabatta on top and serve.

AH! "Make sure not to get cashew butter mixed up with cashew cream. Most of the creams are sweetened, but cashew butter has a neutral taste and can be used for hearty dishes like this one. I don't want to imagine what this baguette would taste like with a sweet cream… In any case, this baguette is soy free; contains lots of healthy fats, vitamins, and polyphenols; and will give you energy for your day—delicious."

SUPER EASY BAGUETTE
with Smoked Tofu, Carrots, and Pesto

INGREDIENTS for 1 baguette (2 servings)

1 bunch flat-leaf parsley

4½ tablespoons olive oil (70 mL)

6½ tablespoons almonds (60 g)

Juice and peel of ½ organic lemon

Sea salt

Freshly ground black pepper

5.5 ounces smoked tofu (150 g)

1 bell pepper

Cinnamon

1 carrot

3¼ cups arugula (80 g)

1 whole grain baguette

PREPARATION TIME: 15 minutes

For the pesto, wash the parsley, shake dry, and coarsely chop the leaves. Purée with 3½ tablespoons (50 mL) olive oil, the almonds, lemon juice, grated lemon peel, sea salt, and pepper in a blender. Cut the smoked tofu into ⅓ inch (3 mm) strips and fry in a skillet in the remaining oil on both sides until crispy. Season with salt and pepper, and then remove from the skillet. Wash the bell pepper, remove the seeds, and cut into thin strips. Pour into a hot skillet, and sauté for 1 minute. Season with 1 pinch of cinnamon and salt and pepper. Peel the carrot, and then use a vegetable peeler to cut into strips. Wash the arugula and spin dry. Cut the whole grain baguette open lengthwise and spread the pesto on the inside of both halves. Layer the bottom half first with the arugula, and then with the bell pepper, smoked tofu, and carrot strips. Place the upper half of the baguette on top. Finished.

AH! This baguette is unbelievably quick to make and is a healthy snack. It's great for school, university, or work, and for when you're on the go. The carrot makes it nice and crunchy."

BLOODY HARRY
Sandwich

INGREDIENTS for 3 sandwiches

Sandwiches:

10.5 ounces tofu (300 g)

3 tablespoons olive oil

Sea salt

Freshly ground black pepper

Some green lettuce leaves (lollo biondo, if it's available)

2 vine-ripened tomatoes

4 cornichons

9 slices of toast bread

Basil Sauce:

½ onion

⅓ cup vegan mayonnaise (80 g)

2½ tablespoons tomato paste (40 g)

1 tablespoon agave syrup

2 tablespoons freshly chopped basil

1 tablespoon freshly squeezed lemon juice

Grated peel of ¼ organic lemon

Sea salt

Freshly ground black pepper

AH! "This sandwich is very quick to make, it's really light (you don't always have to eat whole grain bread), and it tastes great. I consciously chose not to toast the bread for these sandwiches—just like the Americans, who make some of the best sandwiches in the world. That way the texture is nicer in your mouth. If you prefer, you can also serve the sandwiches in the classic triangle shape."

PREPARATION TIME: 30 minutes

Cut the tofu into slices that are almost ½ inch (1 cm) thick and then cut into circles. Heat the olive oil in a skillet and fry the tofu on each side approx. 3 minutes. Season with sea salt and pepper. Wash the lettuce leaves and vine-ripened tomatoes. Thinly slice the tomatoes. Allow the cornichons to drain and thinly slice.

For the sauce, peel and finely chop the onion. Mix with the mayonnaise, tomato paste, agave syrup, basil, and lemon juice and peel. Season with salt and pepper. If you have more time, you can also make the vegan mayonnaise yourself (See the potato salad recipe on page 84). Cut the toast bread into circles. Then assemble the sandwiches as follows: put some lettuce and basil sauce on 3 slices of bread, then layer on 1 more slice of toast, the cornichons, tofu circles, tomato slices, and some more basil sauce. Place a slice of toast on top of each sandwich.

TURKISH PIZZA
with Mint Yogurt Dip

INGREDIENTS for 4 pizzas

Pizza Dough:

¾ cube fresh yeast or 1½ packages

dry yeast

1 level teaspoon raw cane sugar

2 cups first clear flour (250 g)
(If not available, you can use bread flour.)

1 level teaspoon sea salt

Toppings:

7 ounces tofu (200 g)

3½ tablespoons olive oil (50 mL)

2 red onions

2 garlic cloves

6½ tablespoons tomato paste (100 g)

1 tablespoon raw cane sugar

6½ tablespoons dry red wine (100 mL)

Sea salt

Freshly ground black pepper

Cinnamon

⅓ cup pine nuts (50 g)

Mint Yogurt Dip:

2¼ cups soy yogurt (500 g)

Fresh mint (as desired)

Juice and grated peel of

½ organic lemon

3 tablespoons olive oil

Sea salt

Freshly ground black pepper

Filling:

Some lettuce leaves

½ cucumber

2 tomatoes

1 onion

PREPARATION TIME: 30 minutes plus 45 minutes rising time and 5 minutes bake time

Preheat the oven to 480°F (250°C). For the dough, combine the yeast with just under ⅔ cup (140 mL) lukewarm water, and raw cane sugar, and allow to rest in a warm spot for 15 minutes. Then add the flour and sea salt and knead well until the dough is smooth and elastic. Allow to rest in a warm spot for another 30 minutes. In the meantime, mash the tofu with a fork. Heat the olive oil to a high temperature in a non-stick skillet and fry the tofu for 6 minutes. Peel and finely chop the onions and garlic. Add both to the tofu and sauté for 3 more minutes. Fold in the tomato paste and raw cane sugar and let caramelize for 2 minutes. Deglaze with red wine and allow to thicken for 3 minutes. Season with sea salt, pepper, and 2 pinches of cinnamon. Fold in the pine nuts. Divide the dough into four parts, and on a well-floured work surface, roll each one into a circle. Place on baking sheets lined with parchment paper. Spread 3 tablespoons of the tofu mixture on each pizza and press down into the dough with your hands. Bake in the oven for about 5 minutes. Whisk the soy yogurt until creamy. Wash the mint, shake dry, finely chop, and fold into the yogurt mixture along with the olive oil and grated lemon peel and juice. Salt and pepper. Wash the lettuce, cucumber, and tomatoes. Thinly slice the cucumber and tomatoes. Peel the onion and cut into rings. Top the pizzas with the lettuce, cucumbers, tomatoes, and onions. Pour the dip on top, roll up the pizzas, and serve wrapped in parchment paper.

Healthy indulgence without feeling guilty? You might think that's impossible. The different diets that are popular change as often as fashion does; today it's the Atkins diet with a lot of protein and meat, and tomorrow it'll be a cabbage soup diet that's guaranteed to help quickly. A few years ago, I weighed more than 230 pounds (105 kilograms) and had tried many different diets to lose weight. I remember trying a vegetable juice diet. After 48 hours, I couldn't stand it anymore and gorged on a big plate of pasta and bacon. The result was of course as expected: I didn't lose a single ounce.

Not long after that, I started to eat vegan. The pounds began to melt away by themselves. The benefits of this diet when losing weight are obvious: by eating a plant-based diet, you take in a lot more fiber, less saturated fat, and more vitamins. And then you stay satisfied longer. If you want to lose weight, I recommend at least eating whole grain products made with whole wheat flour because you'll feel satisfied longer. These are actually always the better choice because they contain more vitamins and minerals. However, I would never give up my spaghetti made from durum wheat because I simply like it too much. I also don't replace my baguette with a wholegrain alternative when I'm in the mood to have a baguette. But whole grain products today are already in many cases truly a delicious alternative.

As you read more about this topic, you'll become more appreciative of a vegan diet. My first salad dressing was comprised of oil and a premade salad mix—it was terrible! Over the years, I've developed lots of delicious salad recipes that are quick and easy to make, but are also artistic and can be made into a main meal. Shakes and smoothies have also become an important part of my diet— just put fresh fruit, agave syrup, and ice cubes in the blender, turn it on, and you're done! Eating fruit as an ice-cold smoothie tastes great. And that way, I easily get my recommended 2 cups of fruit each day.

LIGHT
and Delicious

MAKI SUSHI

INGREDIENTS for 6 rolls

6 pieces (approx. 3 servings)

Rice:

1¼ cups sushi rice (250 g)

½ teaspoon sea salt

½ tablespoon agave syrup

1 tablespoon white wine vinegar

Filling:

1–2 carrots

½ cucumber

1–2 avocados

7 ounces smoked tofu (200 g)

Oil for frying

Some soy sauce

In addition:

6 nori sheets

Black sesame seeds

Organic wasabi paste

Organic pickled ginger slices

AH! "It's worth trying out different brands of nori sheets because they vary quite a bit."

PREPARATION TIME: 30 minutes

In a saucepan, wash the sushi rice with cold water and allow to drain well in a sieve. Then pour back into the saucepan with just over 2 cups (500 mL) of water (If this differs from the package instructions, use the amount indicated on the package) and a little sea salt. Bring to a boil and simmer over low heat approx. 10 minutes, stirring occasionally, until the rice is tender. Sushi rice should be sticky! Mix with the agave syrup and white wine vinegar. For the filling, peel the carrot and cucumber and cut both into pieces that look like matchsticks. Halve and peel the avocado, remove the pit, and cut into matchstick pieces. Cut the smoked tofu into matchsticks as well and fry the tofu in a skillet in oil with some soy sauce for about 4 minutes on each side. Place a nori sheet on a sushi bamboo mat. Spread ⅙ of the rice out evenly so that it makes a layer that's almost ¼ inch (5 mm). Leave about a 1-inch (2 cm) border on the upper edge and moisten this area with water. Place ⅙ of the carrots, cucumber, avocado, and smoked tofu in the middle and then roll up the nori sheet tightly using the bamboo mat. Press the moistened end against the nori roll. With a very sharp knife, cut the roll into 6 pieces. Do the same with the remaining sheets of nori. Arrange the maki sushi on a plate and sprinkle the sesame seeds on top. Serve with soy sauce, wasabi paste, and pickled ginger.

VEGETABLE COCONUT CURRY
with Basmati Rice

INGREDIENTS for 2 servings

¾ cup Basmati rice (150 g)

Sea salt

1 carrot

1½ cups sugar snap peas (150 g)

1 red chili pepper

1 cup mung bean sprouts (80 g)

3 tablespoons canola oil

1–2 tablespoons soy sauce

1 onion

1 garlic clove

⅓–½ inch fresh ginger (1 cm)

1 teaspoon curry powder

1 cup coconut milk (250 mL)

1 teaspoon agave syrup

¼ bunch cilantro

PREPARATION TIME: 30 minutes

Cook the Basmati rice according to the package instructions in lightly salted water. In the meantime, peel the carrot and cut into thin matchsticks. Wash the sugar snap peas and blanch in well-salted boiling water. Wash the chili pepper, remove the seeds, and cut into thin rings. Wash the mung bean sprouts and allow to drain. Heat 2 tablespoons canola oil in a skillet or wok and sauté the vegetables over high heat for 3 minutes. Add the soy sauce and remove from heat. For the sauce, peel and finely chop the onion, garlic, and ginger. Heat 1 tablespoon canola oil in a skillet; sauté the onions, garlic, and ginger with the curry powder for 2 minutes. Add the coconut milk and agave syrup. Cook for 2 more minutes and season with sea salt. Wash the cilantro, shake dry, finely chop the leaves, and fold into the rice. Arrange the rice on plates with the vegetables and sauce and serve.

AH! This is an Asian inspired rice vegetable dish—light, a bit spicy, and delicious! It's important to remember that not everyone likes cilantro. But if you use it sparingly, it's really tasty. Alternatively, you can use parsley."

SPINACH QUINOA

INGREDIENTS for 1–2 servings

1 red onion

1 garlic clove

4 tablespoons olive oil

¾–1 cup quinoa (150 g)

¾ cup dry white wine (175 mL)

Sea salt

Freshly ground black pepper

2 cups baby spinach (60 g)

½ cup almonds (70 g)

In addition:

Dried apricot pieces

Raisins

AH! "You can use quinoa, which is known as the Incan grain, as rice. It has a very nice texture in your mouth. And it contains a higher amount of protein, magnesium, and iron than the more common types of grains do. The Incas had many uses for quinoa, including using it for sore throats. By the way, apparently it became well known that spinach is rich in iron because of a comma mistake made by a scientist named Dr. E. von Wolf. But the iron in quinoa makes up for the smaller amount of iron in spinach. And even if it should turn out that quinoa doesn't have as much iron as people once thought—as happened with spinach—it still tastes really delicious!"

PREPARATION TIME: 25 minutes

Peel and finely chop the onion and garlic. Heat the olive oil in a large skillet and sauté the onion and garlic for about 2 minutes. Add the quinoa and sauté over high heat for 2 more minutes. Deglaze with the white wine, and stirring constantly, cook over high heat approx. 4 minutes until the sauce has thickened. Add 1¼ cups (300 mL) of water and allow to come just to a boil. Reduce the heat to medium and allow the quinoa to simmer an additional 10–15 minutes, stirring constantly. The quinoa is done when you can no longer see a white kernel inside, and it's still slightly firm to the bite. Season with sea salt and pepper. In the meantime, wash the baby spinach, allow to drain briefly, add to the skillet, and cook until it collapses. Coarsely chop the almonds and add to the quinoa. Serve the spinach quinoa in bowls. You can make the dish a bit more refined by adding dried apricot pieces or raisins. I don't prefer the latter, but many people really like this dish with raisins.

COUSCOUS SALAD

INGREDIENTS for 2 servings

1 onion

1 red bell pepper

½ red chili pepper (as desired)

2 avocados

¼ bunch parsley

¼ bunch mint

1¼ cups couscous (200 g)

3 tablespoons olive oil

Sea salt

Freshly ground black pepper

Lemon or orange juice
(as desired)

PREPARATION TIME: 20 minutens

Peel and finely chop the onion. Wash the bell pepper and chili pepper and remove the seeds from both. Cut the bell pepper into small cubes and the chili pepper into thin slices. Halve and peel the avocados and remove the pits. Cut the avocado pulp into cubes. Wash the herbs, shake dry, and finely chop the leaves. Prepare the couscous according to the package instructions. Mix together with the ingredients you prepared and the olive oil. Season with sea salt, pepper, and a dash of lemon or orange juice.

AH! "This salad is perfect to take with you to the lake, university, or a fast-food restaurant, where you can simply transfer it to one of the plastic containers when nobody is looking :-), so as not to draw attention to yourself."

ASPARAGUS SALAD
with Maple Syrup Mustard Dressing and Arugula

INGREDIENTS for 2 servings

½ small bunch white or green
asparagus (200 g)
Sea salt
Juice and peel of 1½ organic oranges
3 additional oranges
2 teaspoons medium-hot mustard or
Dijon mustard
4 tablespoons olive oil
2 teaspoons maple syrup
Freshly ground black pepper
4 cups arugula (100 g)
½ cup walnuts (50 g)

PREPARATION TIME: 15 minutes

Peel the asparagus and cut off the wooden ends. In a medium-size saucepan, bring just over 3⅓ cups (800 mL) water, 1 teaspoon sea salt, and the juice and peel of 1 organic orange to a boil. Cook the asparagus in this mixture over high heat approx. 12 minutes. In the meantime, use a sharp knife to completely remove the peel from the 3 oranges. Then cut out the orange slices, removing the membranes. For the dressing, mix the mustard, olive oil, and maple syrup. Season with sea salt and pepper. Allow the asparagus to drain and then cut into bite-size pieces. Wash the arugula and spin dry. Carefully mix the asparagus and arugula with the walnuts, orange slices, and dressing. Ciabatta bread goes well with this salad.

AH! "You can get fresh asparagus from the end of April until about the end of June. You'll know it's fresh if it squeaks when you rub the stalks together. It'll stay fresh longer if you store it in damp newspaper."

TOFU CHEF SALAD
with Avocado Dressing

INGREDIENTS for 2 servings

3.5–7 ounces tofu (100–200 g)

3 tablespoons canola oil

3 tablespoons peanut butter (50 g)

2 tablespoons agave syrup

3½ tablespoons soy sauce (50 mL)

Hot chili powder (as desired)

½ teaspoon curry powder

5.5 ounces organic mixed greens
(150 g) (e.g., Lamb's lettuce, arugula, radicchio)

1 carrot

6 cherry tomatoes

1 avocado

1 garlic clove

5–8 tablespoons olive oil

Juice of ½ lemon

Freshly ground black pepper

Sea salt

4½ tablespoons cashews (40 g)

AH! "For this recipe, you should use firm or extra-firm tofu. You can decide for yourself how many tofu pieces you want to make. You should give the tofu pieces time to cool down before you put them on the salad. They also taste great as a snack!"

PREPARATION TIME: 15 minutes

First slice the tofu, and then cut into blocks that are just under ½ inch (1 cm). Heat the canola oil in a skillet and fry the tofu for 5–8 minutes over high heat—making sure that the oil doesn't smoke. Mix the peanut butter, agave syrup, soy sauce, chili powder, and curry powder to a seasoning that still has a bit of liquid. Add the tofu to the skillet, immediately reduce the temperature, mix well, and allow to caramelize approx. 30 seconds. Transfer the tofu blocks to a plate lined with paper towels to drain and then let cool. Wash the mixed greens and spin dry. Peel and grate the carrot. Wash and quarter the cherry tomatoes. For the dressing, halve and peel the avocado, remove the pit, and cut the avocado pulp into small cubes. Peel the garlic and pass through a garlic press. Mix the olive oil with the lemon juice, garlic, and avocado; season with salt and pepper. Mix the salad, carrot, and tomatoes with the dressing and garnish with the tofu blocks and cashews. Bread goes well with this salad.

SANDWICH SPREADS

A. Chickpeas & Tomato

INGREDIENTS for 1 jar
(just over ¾ cup or 200 mL)

1¼ cups canned chickpeas (200 g)

⅓ cup tomato paste (80 g)

3 tablespoons olive oil

1 teaspoon dried oregano

1 level teaspoon sea salt

Freshly ground black pepper

PREPARATION TIME: 10 minutes

Allow the chickpeas to drain. In a skillet, toast the tomato paste in hot oil for 3 minutes. Purée the chickpeas, tomato paste, oregano, sea salt, and 3½ tablespoons (50 mL) water. Season with pepper.

B. Sunflower Seeds & Watercress

INGREDIENTS for 1 jar
(just over ½ cup or 150 mL)

1–1¼ cups sunflower seeds (150 g)

1 tablespoon freshly squeezed lemon juice

1 level teaspoon sea salt

Freshly ground black pepper

1 container of living watercress

PREPARATION TIME: 5 minutes

Purée the sunflower seeds in a blender with just over 1 cup (130 mL) water, lemon juice, and sea salt. Season with pepper. Cut the watercress leaves from the stem, finely chop, and fold in to the mixture.

C. Mint & Peas

INGREDIENTS for 1 jar
(1¼ cups or 300 mL)

2 cups frozen peas (250 g)

Sea salt

⅓ cup pine nuts (50 g)

1 red onion

7 tablespoons olive oil

½ bunch fresh mint

Freshly ground black pepper

PREPARATION TIME: 15 minutes

Cook the peas in well-salted boiling water for 7 minutes. Toast the pine nuts in a dry non-stick skillet for 3 minutes. Remove from heat. Peel and finely chop the onion. Heat 2 tablespoons olive oil in a skillet and sauté the onions for 3 minutes. Wash the mint, shake dry, and finely chop. Purée with the peas, 5 tablespoons olive oil, and 1 level teaspoon salt. Season with pepper and fold in the onions and toasted pine nuts.

MATCHA SHAKE

A. Matcha Shake
B. Power Shake (For recipe, see p. 126)
C. Attila's Energy Drink (For recipe, see p. 127)

INGREDIENTS for 2 servings

2–2 ¼ cups oat milk (500 mL)

3 tablespoons agave syrup

1 level teaspoon matcha
(green tea powder, available in organic grocery stores or on the internet)

½ teaspoon ground vanilla

2 scoops of Vanilla Cashew Ice Cream
(For recipe, see p. 166)

PREPARATION TIME:

5 minutes plus 10 minutes in the freezer

Mix all ingredients well in a blender. Pour into glasses and then put into the freezer for 10 minutes. Add 1 scoop of Vanilla Cashew Ice Cream to each glass and serve immediately.

AH! "Matcha is a finely ground green tea, which is very rich in antioxidants. It was the cult drink of the Samurai. They foamed the tea up in hot water and drank it to help prepare them for battle since they knew that matcha strengthens a person's ability to concentrate. My Western variety is a shake that will help prepare you for "battles" at the office."

Power
SHAKE

(Photo on p. 126)

INGREDIENTS for 2–3 shakes

2 frozen bananas (200 g)

1½ cups frozen blueberries (200 g)

1¾ cups frozen raspberries (200 g)

2½ cups oat milk (600 mL)

1½ teaspoons ground vanilla

5.5 ounces silk tofu (150 g)

3–6 tablespoons agave syrup

Seasonal fruit

2 small skewers

PREPARATION TIME: 5 minutes

Finely purée each of the different types of frozen fruit separately with just over ¾ cup (200 mL) oat milk, ½ teaspoon vanilla, and ⅓ of the silk tofu (50 g) in a blender. Sweeten each shake with 1–2 tablespoons of agave syrup. Wash the seasonal fruit and sort out any that are damaged. Cut into bite-sized pieces that are all about the same size. Layer the 3 shakes in 2 glasses and garnish with the fruit skewers.

AH! "This is a healthy protein shake that is decoratively filled into glasses in three layers. The shake has a lot of vitamins, minerals, and antioxidants that protects the body from free radicals."

Attila's
ENERGY DRINK

(Photo on p. 124)

INGREDIENTS for 2 servings

1 one-half inch cube fresh ginger (5 g)

1 organic lemon

3 bags green tea

6½ tablespoons agave syrup (100 mL)

Ice cubes

PREPARATION TIME: 15 minutes

Peel the ginger and cut into fine slices. Use a vegetable peeler to peel off a thin layer of half of the lemon. Squeeze the juice from the lemon. In a saucepan, bring just over 2 cups (500 mL) of water to a boil. Remove from heat, place the tea bags in the saucepan, and add the remaining ingredients. Let steep for 10 minutes. Pour the tea through a sieve into a second saucepan, and allow to cool. Serve with ice cubes.

AH! "This drink gives me the lasting energy I need for my day and for working out."

I have an incurable sweet tooth and am almost a chocoholic! I can hardly stand a day that doesn't include having something with chocolate! But as the saying goes, first the work, then the pleasure. If you are athletic, do a lot of physical work, or are often on the move, you can reward yourself from time to time. For example, you might treat yourself with a creamy chocolate mousse that is easy to make; pear strudel and pistachio pesto; tiramisu; or a homemade Snicky bar with peanut, cookie, and chocolate layers. All of these recipes are on the following pages.

It's hard to believe that these recipes are vegan. However, cocoa butter is and remains vegan, even if the name sounds a little ambiguous. Incidentally, chocolate contains many good substances that have a mood enhancing effect, and it is rich in antioxidants, which protect your body against free radicals.

Indulging and sinning should be part of what you do since you're already going without animal products. And it's a little less sinful if you use healthier sweeteners like raw cane sugar, natural apple syrup, or agave syrup. A clear advantage of sweet vegan rewards is that they are often lower in fat. Soy whipping cream, for example, only has about 11 percent fat. Cream made from cow milk comes in much worse with 30 percent fat, and it also contains many saturated fatty acids and is high in cholesterol. When I mentioned these advantages at our food photo shooting, Simon our food photographer concluded spontaneously, "Good, now I can finally eat three times as much chocolate mousse!" Naturally, that wasn't quite what I meant.

The low fat content of vegan food is truly one reason why people who follow a vegan diet find it much easier to reach their desired weight and stay there.

SWEET
Rewards

Attila's
CREAM SANDWICHES

INGREDIENTS for about 10 pieces

Cookies:

1⅔ cups all-purpose flour (200 g)

¾ cup raw cane sugar (150 g)

½ cup organic cocoa (60 g)

⅓ cup soft vegetable margarine (80 g)

2 tablespoons soy flour

2 teaspoons baking powder

1 pinch sea salt

1 cup soy milk (250 mL)

Cream Filling:

1¼ cups soy whipping cream (300 mL)
(e.g., Soyatoo!)

¼ cup whipping cream stabilizer (40 g)

6½ tablespoons sugar (80 g)

2 teaspoons freshly squeezed lemon

juice

PREPARATION TIME: 15 minutes plus 8 minutes bake time and 15 minutes cooling time

Preheat oven to 350°F (180°C). Using an electric hand mixer, mix together all of the ingredients for the cookies into a smooth batter. Spread the batter with a spatula to a ⅛ inch (3 mm) thickness on a baking sheet lined with parchment paper. Bake in a hot oven approx. 8 minutes, and then let cool for about 15 minutes. For the cream filling, beat the soy whipping cream with cream stabilizer until stiff while slowly adding the sugar. Fold in the lemon juice. Cut the chocolate rectangle in half. Spread the cream filling evenly on one of the halves, place the other half on top, and then use a sharp knife to cut into about 10 rectangles that are about the same size.

AH! "It's best to store the cream sandwiches in the refrigerator so that the cream stays firm. That is, if there are any sandwiches left to store. I really don't know what sweet snack from my childhood this photo reminds me of. But there was something …"

PEAR STRUDEL
with Pistachio Pesto

INGREDIENTS for 1 strudel

¾ cup all-purpose flour (190 g)

6 tablespoons vegetable oil

1 pinch sea salt

4 pears

5 tablespoons breadcrumbs

½ cup melted vegetable margarine (120 g)

5 tablespoons raw cane sugar

½ cup dried cranberries (100 g) (or raisins)

½ cup pistachios (80 g)

½ cup almond slivers (70 g)

4½ tablespoons agave syrup (70 g)

Powdered sugar

Soy whipping cream (e.g., Soyatoo!)

AH! "Strudel is best if you enjoy it fresh out of the oven served with chilled soy whipped cream or vegan vanilla ice cream. The combination of warm strudel and cold whipped cream or ice cream just can't be beat. You can find larger quantities of organic shelled pistachios fairly cheap on the internet. I always have lots of pistachio on hand at home: for pistachio ice cream or pistachio butter—or, like this recipe for pesto ..."

PREPARATION TIME:

30 minutes plus 10 minutes rising time, 25 minutes bake time and 20 minutes cooling time

Preheat oven to 350° (180°C). Combine the flour, vegetable oil, sea salt and about ⅓ cup (75 mL) water and then knead into a smooth dough. Let rest for 10 minutes. Peel, quarter, and core the pears. Cut the pear quarters into paper-thin (approx. 2 mm) slices. Fry the breadcrumbs in just under ¼ cup (50 g) melted margarine until golden brown. Then mix the pears, breadcrumbs, raw cane sugar, cranberries, 3 tablespoons (30 g) of the pistachios, and 3½ tablespoons (30 g) of the almonds. Roll the dough into a large rectangle (about 21.5 x 17.5 inches or 55 x 45 cm) so that it's paper thin, and then place on a sheet of parchment paper. Spread the filling out along the length of the dough so that it makes a strip that's about 2 inches (5 cm) wide. Leave about 1 inch (3 cm) free on the edges. Generously cover the areas of dough that don't have any filling with the rest of the melted margarine. Fold the edges of the dough in and carefully roll the whole thing into a large roll. If desired, coat the dough with the melted margarine again. Bake in a hot oven for 25 minutes. In the meantime, coarsely chop ⅓ cup (50 g) pistachios in a blender and mix with the agave syrup to make the pesto. Allow the pear strudel to cool, dust with powdered sugar, and spread the pesto along the top. Serve with whipped cream.

CRÈME BRÛLÉE

Classic Crème Brûlée

INGREDIENTS for 4 servings

2 cups soy milk (500 mL)

1½ pkgs. vanilla pudding mix (not the instant variety)

9 tablespoons raw cane sugar

1¼ cups cold soy whipping cream (300 mL) (e.g., Soyatoo!)

AH! "I tried this recipe out for the first time after I saw the movie *Amélie* with Audrey Tatou,. It turned out good the first time."

PREPARATION TIME:

25 minutes plus 45 minutes cooling time

Stir between ⅓ and ½ cup (100 mL) soy milk together with the vanilla pudding mix and 5 tablespoons raw cane sugar together until smooth. Bring the remaining soy milk to a boil in a saucepan, remove from heat, and whisk in the pudding mix. Bring to a boil again briefly, while stirring, and then allow the pudding to cool off at room temperature. Finally, put the pudding in the refrigerator for 30 minutes. Beat the soy whipping cream until stiff and then fold into the pudding one spoon at a time. Fill the cream into 4 shallow bowls (Diameter: 3 inches or 8 cm), and use a spoon to spread it out smoothly. Sprinkle 1 tablespoon raw cane sugar evenly over each serving and caramelize with a crème brûlée torch.

Dark Coconut Crème Brûlée

INGREDIENTS for 4 servings

¾ cup coconut milk (200 mL)

5½ rounded tablespoons raw cane sugar

1½ pkgs. vanilla pudding mix (not the instant variety)

1¼ cups cold soy whipping cream (300 mL) (e.g., Soyatoo!)

3.0 ounces dark vegan chocolate spread (80 g)

PREPARATION TIME:

25 minutes plus 45 minutes cooling time

Stir 3½ tablespoons (50 mL) coconut milk together with the vanilla pudding mix and 1½ rounded tablespoons raw cane sugar together until smooth. Bring the remaining coconut milk to a boil in a saucepan, remove from heat, and whisk in the pudding mix. Bring to a boil again briefly, while stirring, and then allow the pudding to cool off at room temperature. Finally, put the pudding in the refrigerator for 30 minutes. Beat the soy whipping cream until stiff and then stir into the pudding together with the chocolate spread. Fill the cream into 4 shallow bowls (Diameter: 3 inches or 8 cm), and use a spoon to spread it out smoothly. Sprinkle 1 tablespoon raw cane sugar evenly over each serving and caramelize with a crème brûlée torch.

CRUMBLE
in the Jungle

INGREDIENTS or 2 servings

1 vanilla bean pod

¾ cup cold soy whipping cream
(150 g) (e.g., Soyatoo!)

1⅓ cups soy yogurt (300 g)

8 tablespoons agave syrup

2⅔ cups mixed berries (300 g)
(e.g., raspberries, blueberries, blackberries, and
currants, if necessary, use frozen berries)

6 vegan vanilla sandwich cookies

Mint leaves

PREPARATION TIME: 15 minutes

Cut the vanilla bean pod open lengthwise and scrape out the seeds. Beat the ice-cold soy whipping cream until stiff. Carefully fold in the soy yogurt, vanilla seeds, and 2 tablespoons agave syrup. Wash the berries and sort out any that are damaged. Remove the currants from the vines. Mix the berries with 6 tablespoons agave syrup and allow to marinate for 5 minutes. Put the vanilla sandwich cookies in a plastic bag, tie the bag off, and crumble the cookies using a rolling pin. In glasses, alternately layer the cookie crumbles, berries, and cream yogurt, ending with a layer of fruit. Garnish with mint leaves.

AH! "Agave syrup is a plant-based sweetener that's very low on the Glycemic index."

DONAUWELLE CAKE

INGREDIENTS for 1 sheet cake (approx. 20 pieces)

4 cups and 2 tablespoons oat milk (1 liter)

3 pkgs. vanilla pudding mix

2¼ cups raw cane sugar (450 g)

⅔ cup cold soy whipping cream (150 mL) (e.g., Soyatoo!)

2 jars of morello cherries

1 cup and 1½ tablespoons soft vegetable margarine (250 g)

Sea salt

4 cups all-purpose flour (500 g)

5 teaspoons baking powder (15 g)

4 tablespoons soy flour

5 tablespoons cocoa

9 ounces dark chocolate (250 g) (50% cocoa)

AH! "Instead of making a pudding cream layer, you can also make an authentic vegan butter cream using neutral tasting organic margarine. But this is often a bit too heavy for me, so I prefer this lighter version. Donauwelle cake tastes especially delicious when it has cooled completely in the refrigerator. It's also a great cake for any summer party."

PREPARATION TIME: 45 minutes plus 30 minutes bake time and 2 hours cooling time

Combine between ⅓ and ½ cup (100 mL) oat milk with the vanilla pudding mix. Bring the remaining oat milk to a boil with 1¼ cups (250 g) raw cane sugar. Whisk the pudding mix in, and bring to a boil again briefly. Set to the side to cool, stirring occasionally so a skin doesn't form. Put the cold pudding into the freezer for 15 minutes. Beat the soy whipping cream and then fold into the cold pudding one spoon at a time. Preheat the oven to 350°F (180°C). Allow the morello cherries to drain in a sieve. Beat the margarine with 1 cup (200 g) raw cane sugar until fluffy. Add the flour, baking powder, soy flour, 1 pinch sea salt, and just under 1¼ cups (290 mL) water, and then beat with an electric hand mixer into a smooth batter. Line the baking sheet with parchment paper and spread out half of the dough evenly. Stir the cocoa into the remaining batter and then spread onto the light-colored batter. Use a fork to make circles in the batter to obtain a marble effect. Distribute the cherries on the cake and press lightly into the batter. Bake approx. 30 minutes in the middle of a hot oven. Allow to cool for 1 hour. Spread the vanilla cream on the cake. Let cool in the refrigerator for 20 minutes. Coarsely chop the chocolate with a knife, and let melt over a water bath. To do this, allow the chocolate to melt in a metal bowl over a water bath that is on medium heat. The bowl shouldn't come into contact with the water bath. Spread the chocolate on top of the cream layer with a spoon or spatula, and make a wavy pattern with a fork. Let cool in the refrigerator for 10 more minutes.

Attila's
CARROT CAKE

INGREDIENTS for 1 round cake (Diameter: approx. 8.5 inches or 22 cm)

1¼ cups cold soy whipping cream (300 mL) (e.g., Soyatoo!)

1½ cups raw cane sugar (300 g)

Approx. 3 carrots (300 g)

1½ cups all-purpose flour (180 g)

2½ cups ground almonds (300 g)

2 tablespoons baking powder (20 g)

Grated peel of 1 organic lemon

Sea salt

½ teaspoon cinnamon

¼ teaspoon ground cloves

10.5 ounces marzipan (300 g)

If desired, 5.5 ounces marzipan (150 g) and organic food coloring (orange and green, for the decoration)

AH! "The carrots in the cake contain a lot of Provitamin A, and are therefore good for your eyes. The marzipan carrots on the cake actually only contain a lot of delicious calories, but they make the cake look really nice."

PREPARATION TIME: 15 minutes plus 60 minutes bake time and approx. 90 minutes cooling time

Preheat the oven to 350°F (180°C). In a large bowl, beat the cold soy whipping cream until stiff. Slowly pour in the raw cane sugar while stirring. Peel and finely grate the carrots. With a whisk, carefully fold the flour, ground almonds, carrots, baking powder, lemon peel, 2 pinches salt, cinnamon, and cloves into the whipped cream. That way it will keep its volume and the cake will be nice and fluffy. Line a springform pan with parchment paper and pour the batter in the pan. Bake in the middle of a hot oven for 60 minutes. After 35 minutes, cover the pan with aluminum foil and then finish baking. Remove from the oven and allow to cool for 90 minutes. When cool, carefully remove the cake from the springform pan. To make a marzipan cover for your cake, roll out 10.5 ounces (300 g) of marzipan on a clean, smooth surface that has been dusted with powdered sugar. Roll out the marzipan to a very thin layer (approx. ½ cm) that is slightly larger than the size of your cake. When you are rolling the marzipan cover out, keep turning it to make sure it doesn't stick to your work surface. Then, slide a rolling pin underneath the marzipan cover to pick it up and place it on top of the cake. Press the top of the marzipan down first, and then ease it around the sides while smoothing it down with your hands. If there are air bubbles, just lift the marzipan cover up a bit and smooth it out. Mix the 5.5 ounces (150 g) of marzipan with the food coloring to make green and orange marzipan. Use this to make little carrots, which give the cake a nice final touch. Bugs Bunny would be proud.

STRAWBERRY CAKE

(Recipe on p. 146)

STRAWBERRY CAKE (Photo on p. 144)

**INGREDIENTS for 1 round cake
(Diameter: approx. 9 inches or 23 cm)**

Cake Layers:

1¼ cups cold soy whipping cream (300 mL) (e.g., Soyatoo!)

1 vanilla bean pod

1⅓ cups and 1 tablespoon all-purpose flour (300 g)

6½ tablespoons canola oil (100 mL)

2 teaspoons baking powder

1 pinch sea salt

1 tablespoon soy flour

1 cup raw cane sugar (200 g)

4½ tablespoons soy milk (70 mL)

Whipping Cream:

3¾ cups soy whipping cream (900 mL) (e.g., Soyatoo!)

4 pkgs. whipping cream stabilizer

Filling:

1 pkg. red organic cake glaze

3 tablespoons raw cane sugar

4½ cups strawberries (500 g)

In addition:

1 cup blanched, sliced almonds (130 g)

AH! "Try varying the amount of whipping cream stabilizer and only use as much that you need. Some people like the cream to be a little stiffer, while others like it more fluffy. When you are beating the whipping cream, simply add the stabilizer gradually and stop to taste the whipped cream a few times. You should be able to find vegan red cake glaze made without cochineal dye (obtained from crushed insects) in an organic grocery store or on the internet."

PREPARATION TIME: 30 minutes plus 40 minutes bake time and 50 minutes cooling time (cake layers should cool overnight)

Preheat the oven to 350°F (180°C). Beat the soy whipping cream with an electric hand mixer. Cut the vanilla bean pod open lengthwise, scrape out the seeds, and add to the whipped cream. Put in the refrigerator for several minutes. Then, fold in the rest of the ingredients for the cake layers one spoon at a time, stirring after each addition. Pour into a springform pan lined with parchment paper and bake in the middle of a hot oven for 40 minutes. Cover with parchment paper 10 minutes before the end of the bake time. Allow to cool completely—it's best to let it cool overnight! After the cake is cool, cut it into two layers. Place the bottom layer back in the springform pan. For the whipping cream, beat the soy whipped cream with the whipping cream stabilizer until stiff and then put in the refrigerator for 30 minutes. In a saucepan, combine the cake glaze with just over 1 cup (250 mL) water and the raw cane sugar and cook according to the package instructions. Set about 6 strawberries to the side for decorating. Wash, clean, and halve the remaining strawberries and distribute them on the bottom cake layer. Allow everything to cool in the refrigerator for 20 minutes. Remove the ring from the springform pan and spread ⅓ of the cream evenly on top of the strawberries. Place the second cake layer on top and spread half of the remaining cream on it and on the sides of the cake. Put the rest of the cream in a pastry bag and pipe 12 cream swirls onto the cake. Cut the strawberries that you set aside in half and place on top of the cream swirls. Toast the sliced almonds in a dry skillet until they take on a little color. Let cool and then cover the sides of the cake evenly with the sliced almonds.

YOGURT MANDARIN CAKE

INGREDIENTS for 1 round cake (Diameter: approx. 9 inches or 23 cm)

Cake Layers:

1¼ cups soy whipping cream (300 mL) (e.g., Soyatoo!)

1 vanilla bean pod

1⅓ cups and 1 tablespoon all-purpose flour (300 g)

6½ tablespoons canola oil (100 mL)

2 teaspoons baking powder

1 pinch sea salt

1 tablespoon soy flour

1 cup raw cane sugar (200 g)

4½ tablespoons soy milk (70 mL)

Filling:

2¾–3 cups canned mandarins (700 g)

4½ cups soy yogurt (1 kg)

3 tablespoons raw cane sugar

4 level teaspoons agar agar

In addition:

⅓–½ cup canned mandarins (100 g)

AH! "In the last few years, the vegan alternatives available to replace dairy products have really expanded and improved. For example, there is a wide range of soy yogurts. You'll want to try several varieties to see which kind you like the best. If you are planning to use soy yogurt for tzatziki, you should be careful. Some brands of soy yogurt are lightly flavored with sugar and vanilla, which wouldn't taste so great in tzatziki."

PREPARATION TIME: approx. 30 minutes plus 40 minutes bake time and 2 hours cooling time (cake layers should cool overnight)

Preheat the oven to 350°F (180°C). Beat the soy whipping cream with an electric hand mixer. Cut the vanilla bean pod open lengthwise, scrape out the seeds, and add to the whipped cream. Put in the refrigerator for several minutes. Then, fold in the rest of the ingredients for the cake layers one spoon at a time, stirring after each addition. Pour into a springform pan lined with parchment paper and bake in the middle of a hot oven for 40 minutes. Cover with parchment paper 10 minutes before the end of the bake time. Allow to cool completely—it's best to let it cool overnight! For the filling, allow the mandarins to drain in a sieve for 10 minutes and collect the mandarin juice to use later. Cut the cake into two layers. Place the ring of the springform pan around the bottom cake layer again. Distribute ¾ of the mandarins on the bottom cake layer. Whisk together the soy yogurt and the raw cane sugar. In a small saucepan, stir together just over ¾ cup (200 mL) mandarin juice and the agar agar, bring to a boil, and allow to cook for 2 minutes. Whisk into the yogurt mixture and pour half of this mixture on top of the mandarins. Let cool in the refrigerator for 20 minutes. Remove the springform ring, place the second cake layer on top, and spread the remaining yogurt cream on it and on the sides of the cake. Let the cake sit in the refrigerator for 2 hours to allow the flavors to meld. Garnish with the mandarins to serve.

ALMOND WALNUT TRIANGLES

INGREDIENTS for approx.

6 triangles

½ cup walnuts (60 g)

⅓–½ cup blanched, sliced almonds (60 g)

¾–1 cup raw cane sugar (170 g)

1 dark chocolate bar (3.5-ounce) (100 g) (50% cocoa)

PREPARATION TIME: 30 minutes

Coarsely chop the walnuts. Roast the sliced almonds in a dry non-stick skillet until golden brown and then remove from the skillet. Pour the raw cane sugar into the skillet and allow it to caramelize. When the sugar melts, fold in the sliced almonds and walnuts and immediately pour onto a baking sheet lined with parchment paper. Spread the mixture out evenly using a wooden spoon and let it cool. The mixture will cool quickly! When it is cool, use a serrated knife to cut into 6 triangles. Melt the dark chocolate over a water bath. To do this, pour some water in a saucepan and bring to a boil. Turn the heat down to medium, put a metal bowl containing the chocolate on top of the saucepan, and allow the chocolate to melt. The metal bowl shouldn't come into contact with the water bath. Dip half of each walnut triangle into the chocolate and then let cool on a baking rack or on a piece of baking paper.

AH! "It really doesn't matter how big you make the triangles. Make them however you like them the most!"

PANNA COTTA
with Caramel Sauce

INGREDIENTS for 8 servings

3 cups soy cream (700 mL)

1 level teaspoon agar agar (2 g)

1 cup raw cane sugar (220 g)

1 teaspoon ground vanilla

¾–1 cup raspberries (100 g)

AH! "I tinkered with this recipe for a long time until I got perfect results. You need to use exactly 2 grams agar agar—and not one gram more or less. If you use too much, it won't taste that good. It's best to measure the agar agar using a precision scale. The rough conversion is 2 grams equals 1 level teaspoon. Don't use soy whipping cream for this recipe, but rather soy cooking cream. Oat cream also works well or you can use 50% soy cream and 50% oat cream."

PREPARATION TIME: 30 minutes plus 30–60 minutes cooling time

For the panna cotta, whisk just over 2 cups (500 mL) soy cream, 3 tablespoons (40 g) raw cane sugar, the agar agar, and ground vanilla well. In a small saucepan, carefully bring to a boil while stirring, reduce the heat, and allow to simmer for 5 minutes. Pour the mixture immediately into 8 heat-resistant custard cups (each should hold about ⅓ cup or 80 mL), and let cool in the refrigerator for 30–60 minutes. For the caramel sauce, allow the remaining raw cane sugar to caramelize in a skillet over high heat while stirring. Add just over ¾ cup (200 mL) soy cream and stir until the caramelized sugar dissolves. Sort out any damaged raspberries. Take the custard cups out of the refrigerator, and briefly dip into hot water to loosen the panna cotta from the glass edges. That way the panna cotta will fall onto the dessert plates better. Serve with caramel sauce and raspberries.

Crunchy Chocolate
CRANBERRY DROPS

INGREDIENTS

for approx. 15–20 drops

7 ounces dark chocolate (200 g)
(50% cocoa)

1 vanilla bean pod

1⅓ cups cornflakes (50 g)

½ cup dried cranberries (70 g)

PREPARATION TIME: 25 minutes

Coarsely chop the dark chocolate with a knife and then melt over a water bath. To do this, bring some water to a boil in a saucepan. Turn the heat down to medium, put a metal bowl containing the chocolate on top of the saucepan, and allow the chocolate to melt. The metal bowl shouldn't come into contact with the water bath. Cut the vanilla bean pod open lengthwise and scrape out the seeds with a knife. Fold the vanilla seeds and cornflakes into the melted chocolate. Stir in the cranberries. Use 2 teaspoons to make drops that are almost 1 inch (2 cm) in diameter. Let cool on parchment paper.

AH! "This is the perfect snack to eat while relaxing on the couch, and it's also healthy. High-quality dark chocolate contains a lot of valuable substances that put us in a good mood, and cranberries are very rich in antioxidants and vitamins. If you don't like cranberries, you can also use raisins, chopped dried apricots, or dates."

CHOCOLATE CROISSANTS
and Quick Strawberry Jam

INGREDIENTS

for approx. 4 croissants

1 pkg. frozen organic whole grain or

classic puff pastry sheets
(10. 5 ounces or 300 g, 6 pastry squares)

3.5 ounces dark chocolate (100 g)
(50% cocoa)

For One Jar Strawberry Jam

(9 ounces or 250 g):

2¼ cups strawberries (250 g)

½ teaspoon agar agar

6½ tablespoons agave syrup (100 mL)

AH! "After you roll the croissants up,
fold the ends towards the middle to
make the classic croissant shape. One
of these croissants and a soy latte is a
great way to start the day."

PREPARATION TIME: 20 minutes plus
30 minutes thawing time, 15 minutes bake time,
and 30 minutes cooling time

Preheat the oven to 350°F (180°C). Let the puff
pastry thaw for about 30 minutes. Place 3 pastry
squares on top of each other and use a rolling
pin to thinly roll them out into a rectangle that is
12 x 6 inches or 30 x 15 cm. Do the same for the
other 3 pastry squares. Cut both large rectangles
diagonally so that you end up with triangles.
Coarsely chop the dark chocolate with a knife.
Sprinkle the chocolate on the shorter sides—leaving
a little space free on the edges—of the pastry
triangles, and then roll each one up from the long
side to the tip. Place on a baking sheet lined with
parchment paper and bake in a hot oven approx.
15 minutes. If you want less work, you can fill and
roll up the puff pastry right out of the box, but then
you'll end up with funny looking mini croissants.
They'll still taste good, though. For the strawberry
jam, wash, clean, and finely purée the strawberries.
Combine the agar agar with 1 tablespoon water
and add this mixture to the strawberries. Boil the
strawberries 5 minutes while stirring, sweeten with
agave syrup as desired, and let cool 30 minutes. The
jam can be stored in the refrigerator for 1–2 days.

ATTINELLO PRALINES

INGREDIENTS

for approx. 36 pieces

10½ ounces white vegan

chocolate (300 g) (organic grocery store or internet)

¾ cup blanched, chopped

almonds (100 g)

2½ tablespoons white almond

butter (40 g)

¼ cup coconut milk (60 mL)

½–⅔ cup unsweetened shredded

coconut (40 g)

PREPARATION TIME:

20 minutes plus 15 minutes cooling time

Melt the white vegan chocolate over a hot water bath. To do this, bring some water to a boil in a saucepan. Put a metal bowl containing the chocolate on top of the saucepan, and allow the chocolate to melt. The metal bowl shouldn't come into contact with the water bath. Add the almonds, almond butter, and coconut milk to the white vegan chocolate and mix well with an electric hand mixer. Then put in the refrigerator for 15 minutes. Use a teaspoon to dole out the praline mixture and roll into balls. Coat the pralines with the shredded coconut.

AH! "I use white rice milk chocolate for this recipe. However, other versions of white vegan chocolate will also work well."

SNICKY BARS

INGREDIENTS

for approx. 36 bars

Cookie Layer:

1¼ cups all-purpose flour (150 g)

1 teaspoon baking powder

7 tablespoons cold vegetable margarine (100 g)

¼ cup raw cane sugar (50 g)

Sea salt

Top Layers:

7.5 ounces dark chocolate (220 g) (50% cocoa)

1⅔ cups crunchy peanut butter (400 g)

4½ tablespoons agave syrup (70 g)

Sea salt

½ teaspoon ground vanilla

⅔ cup shelled peanuts (100 g)

AH! "I'm a cookie monster and I love eating peanuts and chocolate together. It's a combination that just can't be beat. The cookie layer gives this treat the perfect crunch. If the dough is too dry, you can add 2–3 tablespoons of water so that it will hold together better. By the way, ground vanilla (available in small jars in organic grocery stores and online) is made by grinding the entire vanilla bean pod. Using ground vanilla costs less and is simpler than scraping out vanilla bean pods."

PREPARATION TIME: 15 minutes plus 13 minutes bake time and 85 minutes cooling time

Preheat the oven to 350°F (180°C). For the cookie layer, sift the flour and baking powder onto your work surface and form a well in the middle. Cube the margarine and add to the well along with the raw cane sugar, 1 pinch of sea salt, and 2 tablespoons water. Quickly knead the ingredients together into a smooth dough. Form the dough into a ball, wrap in plastic wrap, and cool in the refrigerator for 30 minutes. Place the dough between 2 sheets of parchment papers and roll into a rectangle (approx. 14 x 7 inches or 36 x 18 cm). Place the dough on a baking sheet lined with parchment paper, use a fork to poke several holes in it, and bake in the middle of a hot oven approx. 13 minutes. After baking, allow to cool for 30 minutes. For the top layers, melt the dark chocolate over a water bath. To do this, bring some water to a boil in a saucepan. Turn the heat down to medium, put a metal bowl containing the chocolate on top of the saucepan, and allow the chocolate to melt. The metal bowl shouldn't come into contact with the water bath. Allow to cool for 10 minutes and then use about ⅓ of the chocolate to spread a paper-thin layer on top of the cookie layer. Combine the peanut butter with the agave syrup, 1 pinch of sea salt, and the ground vanilla. Roll this mixture out between 2 sheets of parchment paper so that it's the same size as the cookie layer. Remove one of the sheets of parchment paper and place the nut mixture on top of the cookie layer. Remove the sheet of parchment paper on top, spread the melted chocolate onto the nut mixture, and at the same time, sprinkle peanuts on top of everything. Allow to cool in the freezer for 15 minutes. With a sharp knife, cut into bars that are ¾ inches wide (2 cm) and 3½ inches long (9 cm).

CHOCOLATE AND VANILLA MOUSSE
with Strawberries

INGREDIENTS for 4 servings

7 ounces white rice milk chocolate
(200 g)
(organic grocery store or internet)

7 ounces dark chocolate
(50% cocoa)

2½ cups cold soy whipping cream
(600 mL) (e.g., Soyatoo!)

2⅔ cups strawberries (300 g)

2 vanilla bean pods

2 tablespoons raw cane sugar

AH! "If you want to make both varieties, as shown in the photo, you will need white rice milk chocolate for the white mousse. In Europe, you can get it from Bonvita or Bioart. Many organic grocery stores here don't carry white milk rice chocolate even though it's available to order. And hopefully, it will be available in the States soon. So, I recommend finding this product on the internet and buying enough to last you a while."

PREPARATION TIME: 25 minutes plus 40 minutes cooling time

Chop the white and dark chocolate into small pieces with a knife and melt the two kinds separately over a water bath. To do this, bring some water to a boil in a saucepan. Turn the heat down to medium, put a metal bowl containing the chocolate on top of the saucepan, and allow the chocolate to melt. The metal bowl shouldn't come into contact with the water bath. Then allow to cool for 10 minutes. In the meantime, beat the soy whipping cream until stiff. Using a whisk, fold half of the whipping cream into each of the two types of melted chocolate, and put both in the freezer for 30 minutes so that the mousse can get firm. Wash, clean, and halve the strawberries. Cut the vanilla bean pods open lengthwise and scrape out the seeds. Mix the strawberries with the raw cane sugar and vanilla seeds, and then put the mixture in the refrigerator. Remove the mousse from the freezer, and use two tablespoons to make eggshaped portions. Serve with the marinated strawberries on dessert plates.

Attila's
TIRAMISU

INGREDIENTS for 4 servings

Vanilla Cream:

1½ pkgs. vanilla pudding mix

5 tablespoons raw cane sugar

2 cups soy milk (500 mL)

½ teaspoon ground vanilla

3¼ cups cold soy whipping cream
(300 mL) (e.g., Soyatoo!)

Classic Tiramisu:

Approx. ⅔ cup cold strong coffee
(150 mL)

½ tablespoon raw cane sugar

8 slices zwieback toast

1.5–2 ounces dark chocolate (50 g)
(50% cocoa)

Strawberry Tiramisu:

2⅔ cups strawberries (300 g)

5 tablespoons agave syrup

½ teaspoon ground vanilla

1 cup soy milk (250 mL)

8 slices zwieback toast

2½ tablespoons blanched, sliced
almonds (25 g)

AH! "Classic or strawberry? Both versions
are delicious, so it's best to make the vanilla
cream first and then decide which of the
varieties you prefer. Or you can make a
double batch of vanilla cream and enjoy
both tiramisu versions at the same time."

PREPARATION TIME:

45 minutes plus 40 minutes cooling time
For the vanilla cream, combine the pudding
mix, raw cane sugar, and 6½ tablespoons
(100 mL) soy milk. In a saucepan, bring
1⅔ cups (400 mL) soy milk to a boil and then
remove from heat. Stir in the pudding mixture
and ground vanilla. Bring to a boil again over
high heat while stirring and then let cool
in the refrigerator for 20 minutes. Beat the
refrigerated soy whipping cream until stiff
and fold into the pudding one spoon at a time.
Put the cream into the refrigerator again, this
time for 20 minutes. For the classic tiramisu,
sweeten the coffee with the raw cane sugar.
Set 8 glasses to the side for serving. Dip the
zwieback toast slices in the coffee for a
maximum of 20 seconds. Alternately layer the
vanilla cream and zwieback toast slices in the
glasses. Make chocolate shavings and sprinkle
over the tiramisu. Put in the refrigerator. Wash
and clean the strawberries. Purée 2¼ cups
(250 g) strawberries with 4 tablespoons agave
syrup and the ground vanilla in a blender. Set
8 glasses to the side for serving. Combine
the soy milk with 1 tablespoon agave syrup.
Briefly dip the zwieback toast slices in this
mixture. Alternately layer the zwieback toast
slices and the strawberry purée. Top with the
remaining strawberries and the blanched,
sliced almonds.

PANCAKES
with Berries and Vanilla Cashew Ice Cream

INGREDIENTS for 2 servings

Pancakes:

1¼ cups whole wheat flour (150 g)

1¼ cups soy milk (300 mL)

2 teaspoons baking powder

Sea salt

4 bananas

3 tablespoons vegetable oil

Ice Cream:

2 vanilla bean pods

¾ cup cashew butter (200 g)

15 ice cubes (190 g)

2½ tablespoons agave syrup (35 g)

Sea salt

¾ cup blueberries (100 g)

¾–1 cup strawberries (100 g)

¾–1 cup raspberries (100 g)

3½ tablespoons maple syrup (50 mL)

PREPARATION TIME: 20 minutes

Whisk the whole wheat flour, soy milk, baking powder, and 1 pinch of sea salt together. Peel 2 bananas, cut into small pieces, and fold into the batter. Brush a non-stick skillet with a thin layer of vegetable oil. Use a ladle to pour the batter for each pancake into the skillet, and use the bottom side of the ladle to smooth the pancakes out. Cook the pancakes approx. 3 minutes on each side over medium heat. This recipe makes enough for about 8 pancakes. For the ice cream, cut the vanilla bean pods open lengthwise and scrape out the seeds. Put the vanilla, cashew butter, ice cubes, agave syrup, and 1 pinch of sea salt in a blender, and using the tamper, purée at the highest speed for 1 minute just until the mixture is smooth; you don't want it to turn into a liquid. You can try using a blender that doesn't have a tamper built into the lid, but then you'll have to keep stopping to scrape the ice cream off the sides. Peel the remaining bananas and cut into slices. Wash the berries and sort out any that are damaged. Layer the pancakes and the fruit alternately to make little stacks. Place a scoop of ice cream on the stack and drizzle maple syrup over the top.

AH! "Pancakes are great for breakfast. I had them the first time when I was backpacking in Thailand—they were amazing!"

TIPS

When I look back, I can see that I have gone through several phases of eating vegan and that these were also a part of my personal development. And in each of these phases, my shopping habits also changed. In the beginning, my goal was to cook dishes that were similar to the original meat dishes, and I wasn't yet particularly concerned about the quality of the ingredients I used.

During this first phase, ordinary grocery stores were a good option. However, it was often difficult since many of the products offered contained hidden animal ingredients. For example, I determined that the margarine contained milk powder, the dark chocolate had milk fat in it, and the strawberry ice cream contained a red dye obtained from dead lice, called cochineal. I think it's important to say that I didn't become vegan because of the lice, but rather because of more important reasons such as climate change and my health. But ice cream that has dye made from dead lice in it isn't at all appetizing—regardless of whether or not you're vegan.

It's a lot nicer to shop in an organic grocery store because the products there are clearly labeled and the ingredient lists are usually not so long and complicated. And anyway, the basis of a vegan diet should be fresh fruits and vegetables, grains, legumes, nut butters, and dried fruits—so, you can't go very wrong when shopping vegan. If you like to have an instant cup of soup during the day or like to occasionally eat packaged pasta dishes or other meals that you can put in the microwave, an increasing number of these products that are organic are now being labeled as "vegan." There are now also plenty of great instant vegan snacks that work well for in between meals.

On the next few pages, you'll find some of the most important tips for shopping vegan. I'm not interested in promoting certain products, even if it looks like that at first; I just simply would like to give you tips as to which products and equipment are essential if you want to get good results when cooking vegan. Many items are similar to traditional cooking—other things are really new territory.

You've probably often seen the phrase, "May contain traces of milk (etc.)" on chocolate bars. This is simply a warning for those who have allergies. It means that the vegan chocolate, for example, was produced in the same room where there was perhaps an open milk carton, or that they were made on a machine that was also used to make milk chocolate. However, there would only be a very trace amount of mixing of one chocolate with the other. The manufacturer includes this sentence as a way to protect itself legally. I buy these products with a good conscience.

Vegan
ALTERNATIVES

CREAM

Instead of cooking cream, I most like to use white almond butter, which I mix with water. Almonds are very healthy, contain a lot of calcium, and will make your dish fragrant and slightly sweet. You can also use alternatives such as soy or oat cream. Oat cream isn't yet available in the United States, but hopefully, it will be soon. Soyatoo! is still the only brand of organic whipping cream I know that will give you good results. Some people don't like the light soy taste, but you can get around this by adding flavor. For example, you can add real vanilla or some cocoa powder to make a 2-minute chocolate mousse. There are also other vegetable cream alternatives that are wonderfully suitable for cooking that are based on oats, rice, or soy.

MEAT

If you are making the transition to a vegetarian diet and don't want to give up on hearty, meat-like dishes, it's best to look for alternatives at an organic grocery store. There is a huge selection, and you'll find products such as veggie burgers, vegan gyros, vegan chicken nuggets, and tofu sausages. These products are also great for barbecuing in the summer—but it's very important to brush them with oil; otherwise, they'll turn out a bit dry. The advantages of these alternatives are, of course, that they are produced organically and sustainably, and that they're free from unhealthy animal fats. If you can't go entirely without meat, I would really recommend that you at least buy organic meat. If a great number of people did this, the phenomenon of factory farming wouldn't even exist.

For Bolognese, chili, and chef salad strips, I prefer extra-firm tofu because the main thing here is that the dishes have a meat-like texture. Extra-firm tofu should be very firmly compressed and shouldn't be at all wobbly. If you want to make a tofu cream—such as for a dessert—it's best to use softer types. The degree of compression can be seen in the number of air bubbles the tofu has: soft tofu has lots of air bubbles, firm tofu fewer. It's best to see for yourself. My advice is to just to hold two different blocks of tofu in your hand and compare them. For absolute beginners, I recommend trying flavored varieties of tofu. Look for a good firm smoked tofu. After you find one you like, you'll quickly forget about your fears of tofu or any bad experiences you've had with tofu. Some people like their smoked tofu raw, but I really like it fried, for example, as small cubes or paper-thin slices—that way it gets nice and crisp. Flavored tofu varieties with sun-dried tomatoes, olives, and basil are also good.

EGGS

If you are planning on baking a cake and you need eggs for it, try using soy flour instead. Eggs contain lecithin, which acts as a binding agent. Soy flour contains natural soy lecithin and is a really good replacement. Using soy lecithin has been an industrial standard for a long time as you can see if you look at the ingredient lists on various convenience products such as yogurts and puddings. Incidentally, mashed bananas and applesauce also work well as binders. For whipped egg whites, you can use an egg substitute powder (organic grocery stores, well-stocked supermarkets). You just mix it with water and whisk it with a wire whip until it's foamy. Soy whipping cream is also a good option here.

MILK

Instead of dairy milk, there are a variety of milk substitutes that you can use, such as soy milk, soy-rice blend, oat milk, rice milk, almond milk, and hemp milk. There is also a wide selection of flavors such as vanilla, chocolate, mocha, chai, and strawberry. Again, not all of these are of the same quality. If you've ever had a bad experience with plant-based milk, you should continue to try different varieties until you find one that you like.

CHEESE

Vegan cheese is available at supermarkets, organic grocery stores, and online. However, the quality varies greatly. The taste ranges from smelly feet to plastic to really great tasting, hearty alternatives that work well to substitute cow's milk cheese. My favorites are from Switzerland—what else would you expect from a cheese nation? Today, vegan cheese comes in many different varieties. You can buy grated cheese for pizza, as well as sliced vegan cheese and cheese spreads. And since there is an increased demand for cholesterol-free vegan cheese, I'm optimistic that the selection will only get better.

BUTTER

For butter, there are good substitutes in the supermarket as well as in organic grocery stores and health food stores. You should make sure that the margarine you buy doesn't contain any hydrogenated fats, as these are not healthy. As long as you follow this rule, margarine is healthier than butter. In the U.S., there are lots of great brands to try.

HONEY

I prefer to use raw cane sugar or agave syrup as sweeteners. The latter is a very good alternative to honey. Natural apple syrup and sugar beet syrup are also sweet and a healthy option. For health reasons, I would recommend avoiding industrial sugar as much as you can.

MAYONNAISE

It's well known that mayonnaise is made from eggs, and is therefore not for vegans. However, you can find egg-free mayonnaise in organic grocery stores or health food stores and in some supermarkets in the dry goods aisle. These are made with vegetable oil and thickeners. You can also make your own mayonnaise quickly using soy milk, vegetable oil, vinegar, and locust bean gum. If you have the desire to try it out, you can use the recipe on page 84 in this cookbook (potato salad).

GELATIN

A good substitute for gelatin is agar agar, which is made from algae. If you want to make your own marmalade using fresh fruit, instead of gelatin, you can use pectin, which is extracted from apples and is available in packages at organic grocery stores or you can use agar agar—both give great results! Vitamin capsules are also not always free of animal products; many capsules, such as those for vitamins or green tea extract, are also made from gelatin. This of course is a personal matter of deciding for yourself whether or not you want to buy something like this—I just think it's interesting how widespread the use of animal products is.

SANDWICH SPREADS AND FRUIT DESSERTS

These products often contain bits of ground animal bones. For anyone who isn't eating a completely vegan diet, but is just starting with a few vegetarian days a week, it is certainly interesting to know the facts. Many of the sandwich spreads and fruit desserts available are made with gelatin, which is literally the milled bones of animals. In addition, many of the creams in cream cakes are stabilized with gelatin. It's too bad because agar agar is a vegetable thickener, which could be used instead. By the way: gummy bears also contain gelatin.

PROCESSED FOODS

Processed foods sometimes contain lard. It's very commonly used in conventional products that are in jars or frozen as it allegedly creates a heartier flavor.

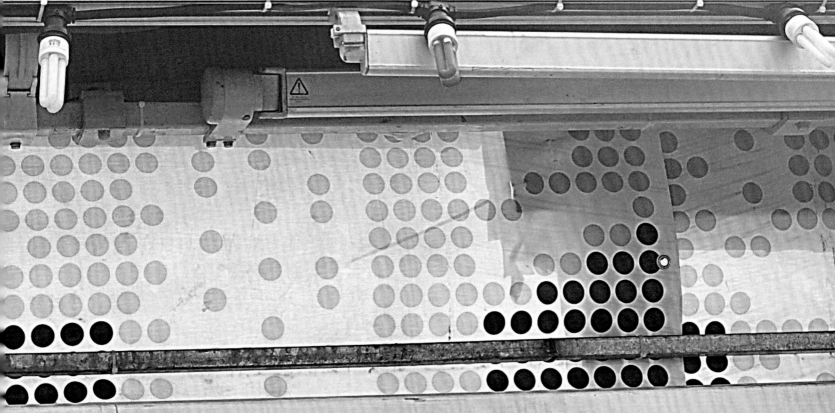

ON THE GO Vegan

It's still quite difficult as a vegan—or even as a vegetarian—to get your money's worth in restaurants. I've heard lots of horror stories and have had several bad experiences of my own. For example, I was at a friend's wedding, where they had gone out of their way to offer a vegan menu and we were enjoying the time until the food came, drinking good wine and chatting with the other wedding guests. Then it arrived: there was salad with sunflower seeds without any dressing as far as we could tell, pasta with butter that definitely wasn't vegan, tossed in a sauce made of unseasoned, peeled tomatoes from a can, alongside frozen vegetables, including crinkle cut carrot slices and peas. When I brought the dish back to the kitchen and asked the chef if he couldn't just make a fresh pesto, he snapped at me: "Get out of my kitchen! We ain't got any pesto." The dessert was also a disaster. There was one finely sliced strawberry, and a slice of pineapple, which had suffered the same fate.

Apart from the fact that many chefs don't even know what vegan means, many of the dishes simply don't taste good and aren't creative. However, there are now some restaurants, particularly in many of the larger cities, that have vegan cuisine as their specialty, and when I eat at these restaurants, I'm always very satisfied. But these are unfortunately the exceptions. It's important to make it clear to the waiter or waitress what you want to order and to explain what vegan is: no meat, no dairy products, and no eggs. You can also make it clear that you want to have something that's not on the menu, or simply ask to combine two dishes—for example, pasta with pesto or tomato sauce, fried potatoes with salad, pasta with garlic and olive oil, bruschetta or sautéed vegetables, and for dessert, a sorbet or fruit salad. But be careful: there are still a few restaurants that sneak in eggs and milk to their pizza dough—which would make any real Italian "Mamma" turn in her grave since the original pizza dough recipe is completely vegan and only calls for flour, water, yeast, salt, and good extra virgin olive oil.

Since the selection is so small, many people today still choose to be flexitarians: vegetarians when they're on the go, vegan when they're at home. I can completely understand that! Or you can speak up and suggest a vegan restaurant where you and your friends or colleagues could eat. Many people are pleasantly surprised afterwards—particularly about how good they feel after a vegan meal.

Kitchen
TOOLS

In my kitchen, I mostly have fresh fruits and vegetables; nut butters; pasta in all imaginable shapes and colors; legumes (either dry or pre-cooked in a can for a quick batch of hummus); antipasti variations such as sun-dried tomatoes, marinated artichoke hearts, and olives; good oils like mild canola oil, olive oil, walnut oil, and pumpkin seed oil; and basics such as polenta (cornmeal), rice, and of course lots of of vegan protein sources like tofu, nuts, and green leafy vegetables.

As for good equipment, I recommend not buying too many different things, but rather a few high-quality kitchen appliances. I have bought many over the years, tried them out, and thrown most of them away because they just weren't any help. It is really important to have a good, sharp knife that isn't too large. I have an all-rounder in my kitchen, which I use to cut up larger things, peel onions, and also chop herbs. I even take the knife with me when I go on TV for a cooking or talk show—you never know what kind of bad equipment might be waiting for you.

BLENDERS

I have had bad experiences with cheap blenders. They have burnt out on me more than once, especially when I tried to purée firmer things like nuts. Since vegan cuisine often relies on nut pastes, and pestos, I recommend that you invest in a professional blender right from the start. For example, if you want to make really delicious ice cream that only requires ice cubes and cashews (Recipe on page 166), you should definitely get a high-power blender such as the Vitamix. It does cost a small fortune, but then you can make peanut butter, sorbets, and ice cream as well as soups and shakes—and with a 2 horsepower motor, it's a real powerhouse. True to the motto: my house, my car, my boat, my 2 horsepower blender!

PRESSURE COOKER

Alongside fresh fruits and vegetables, legumes are also an important pillar of a vegan diet. For cooking legumes, I recommend buying a small pressure cooker with about 2.5 liters capacity. This way you can shorten the cooking time for chickpeas from 3 hours in a normal saucepan down to 25 minutes in a pressure cooker—and the chickpeas turn out a lot more tender.

PEELER

When cooking vegan, you are going to be working a lot with fruits and vegetables. So, you will need to buy a good peeler before you end up frustrated with peeling carrots and decide to throw a steak in the pan instead. I have tried many peelers; my favorite is the "Gourmet" vegetable peeler by WMF. You can order it both in Europe and in the States.

DEEP FRYER

I am a self-confessed fast food junkie; my middle name even used to be "Big Mac." After years of looking for a healthier way to deep fry foods, I came across a fryer called T-fal Actifry, which is also available in Europe and in the States. This is a deep fryer that I use to conjure crispy French fries using only 1 tablespoon of good oil and 500 grams of potatoes. They taste great without it going to your hips.

MISCELLANEOUS

I like to fry and sauté food in Teflon pans because nothing sticks. And you should also have a kitchen scale, a wooden cutting board, a working stove and oven, and an altar beautifully adorned with candles, flower chains, and all the trappings—to set your copy of *Vegan for Fun* on. Oh yeah, the love of good food, creativity, and enjoyment are also important things that should always be a part of your kitchen!

WEBSITES
for Shopping and Reading More

I buy almost everything that I need in organic grocery stores and really hope that if you aren't yet familiar with these that you'll take the opportunity to go and look around in one. Sometimes, you have the opportunity to become a member of the store, and then you can benefit from special member discounts. The selection is always huge and they have both the basics that every vegan should have in their kitchen as well as special alternative products like vegan yogurt, cheese, ice cream, and lots more.

If you would like to get to know more about veganism and healthy eating, I recommend starting with the following websites:

www.rapunzel.de/uk
If you don't have an organic grocery store around the corner, then you can quickly and easily order nut butters and other staples here.

www.wholefoodsmarket.com
Eating foods that contain pesticides isn't a good idea. At Whole Foods, you'll find a huge selection of organic products such as amaranth, tofu, nut butters, and vegan snacks for when you're on the go.

www.aiya-america.com
The supplier for organic matcha! Aiya is Japan's largest matcha producer. The growing region is located far from Fukushima. Remember a day without matcha is a wasted day!

INDEX

THANKS!

A warm thanks to all of the hard-working, hungry employees at **BECKER JOEST VOLK PUBLISHING COMPANY,** who offered to be guinea pigs and cooked all of the recipes in this book. Besides the fact that you did a great job of cooking and eating the dishes, most importantly, you are a super team and I really appreciated your professionalism, Thank you, **MOM,** for your loving support and for not being upset that I stole your crepe recipe and then changed it. Thank you, **DIMI,** for all your love, care, and support in the last few years. We've been through thick and think together—in the truest sense of the word! I'm very thankful that you are who you are! A heartfelt thanks to my **FRIENDS** who still had the energy to stay up until midnight talking with me or to go get a falafel, even after long photo shootings for the cookbook. Thank you, **SIMON** and **JOHANNES.** The days in the food photo studio with you were jam-packed, but also a lot of fun. I still admire Johannes' steady hand as he arranged the food and Simon's humor—and their understanding when the kitchen was a complete mess because of me! Thank you, **SANDRA,** for the fantastic pictures—our photo shootings were really very cool. Thank you, **STEPHANIE,** for editing the recipes. I'm sorry that the amounts given for the tiramisu recipe probably gave you nightmares. Thank you, **JUSTYNA,** for your great layouts. The cover still looks like Mallorca to me even though we were never there. A special thanks to **RALF,** who was often there for me with valuable advice—even for things that didn't have anything to do with cooking. I hope we can include your recipe for tofu with a porcini mushroom and mustard crust in the next cookbook. Thank you, **JOHANNA, CINDY, CLAUDIA, ANNE, ANDREA, MELANIE, ELLEN, ANDREAS,** and all of the other hard-working helpers and test cooks at the publishing company and in my circle of friends. You guys rock! Thank you, **JÜRGEN,** for our productive cooperation and for having the right instinct about which publishing company would be the best for me. It seems like it was just yesterday that we went to eat at a vegan restaurant with Ralf and Justyna from the publishing company and *Vegan for Fun* was only a castle in the air. Thank you for always being a calm presence when we had difficulties at the beginning—I look forward to the continued work together. A special thanks to the entire team at **KICK MANAGEMENT** and especially to **DIANA, KATHRIN, NINA, CHRISTIAN,** and naturally **GOETZ.** And if I've forgotten someone, please don't get upset. It must just be the Vitamin B12 deficiency that's known for causing memory problems. There's one thing that I understood very early studying physics: we are all connected at the atomic level through the magical effects of quantum mechanics—and if the chemistry is right, multiple little particles combine to form a strong molecular bond.

PUBLICATION DETAILS

First published by Becker Joest Volk
Publishing Company
© 2013—all rights reserved
First edition: October 2013
ISBN 978-3-95453-011-3

RECIPES AND TEXT Attila Hildmann
FOOD PHOTOS Simon Vollmeyer
FOOD STYLING Johannes Schalk
PHOTOS Sandra Czerny
LAYOUT, TYPOGRAPHICAL DESIGN Justyna Krzyzanowska for the
publicity agency Makro Chroma Joest & Volk OHG
EDITING OF RECIPES (GERMAN) Dr. Stephanie Kloster (chief editor),
Bettina Snowdown
TRANSLATION Kerstin Gackle
EDITING (ENGLISH) Jason Gackle
PRINTED BY APPL Group, aprinta druck GmbH, Wemding, Germany

FSC
www.fsc.org
MIX
Paper from
responsible sources
FSC® C004592

**BECKER
JOEST
VOLK
VERLAG**

www.bjv-books.com

Vegan for Fun is also available as an e-book on iTunes
or a Kindle version on Amazon.